Captain for Hire

Adventures in Yacht Deliveries

Leo Couturier

To all the crew who ever sailed with me, and to Christine, the first mate in my life.

Published in Canada by Pilot Publishing Canada
www.leocouturier.com

Library and Archives Canada Cataloguing in Publication

Couturier, Leo, 1926–
    Captain for hire : adventures in yacht deliveries / Leo Couturier.

ISBN 0-9739391-0-9

    1. Couturier, Leo, 1926–. 2. Couturier, Leo, 1926– —Travel.
3. Yachting. 4. Sailors — Canada — Biography. I. Title.

GV810.92.C68A3 2006   623.88'223   C2005-907861-8

Printed in Canada

ACHNOWLEDGEMENTS

Along the way, I discovered that I loved sailing as much as I liked diving when I was a kid in Canada. Now I've recently discovered that I love writing as much as I loved sailing. The people I've met during my efforts to get here—people who are champions in their own field—have made writing for me just as enjoyable as the many wonderful people I met while voyaging around the world made sailing. So many thanks to my marvelous editor, Marie-Lynn Hammond; David E. Howard for his nautical knowledge; Bill Hushion, for his encouragement; Nicholas Boothman, for persuading me in less than 90 seconds to write this book; Jack Steiner, for the design and production of this book; and Christine, for her patience.

Without their help and contributions, this book would never have surfaced on any bookshelf.

TABLE OF CONTENTS

Foreword

Here's the big question: how do you get to sail to exotic destinations all over the world on beautiful yachts and get paid for doing so?

This book answers that question. I started off as a mere boat repairman in a boatyard, occasionally relocating boats for a yacht broker and yacht owners. I ended up with a full-time career spanning four decades, moving yachts on four continents. The boats ranged from 25 to 156 feet long, and some featured as many as six crew members. I hope this book will be an inspiration to any sailors or would-be sailors pondering the feasibility of a life on the water. My goal is to both entertain you and provide the relevant information you need to get you on a boat and help you embark on your own successful career.

Leo Couturier,
December 2005

Rising to the America's Cup Challenge

 In 1972 I and my niece Diane sailed in my boat, the *Mal de Terre*, to Guatemala, where we visited friends, cruised on lakes, rode a dinghy down the Oscuro River and explored Indian villages. After a 10-week trip, we finally headed for home, which for me at that time was Fort Lauderdale. Departing from the Caribbean-flavored town of Livingston on Guatemala's east coast, we sailed with a fair wind and a good current in our favor. Resisting the temptation to stop again at the places we had visited on the way down, we kept going till we reached Miami.

After arriving at the Miami Bayside Marina, I needed to call Customs. The only public phone available was being used by a man having a heated argument with someone about a transmission problem forcing him to cancel his trip to the Bahamas. When he hung up, he said to me, "Sorry I kept you waiting. We were heading to the islands when the transmission broke down and my mechanic says he's busy on another boat." He was a tall, athletic type, with a friendly smile in spite of his troubles. While he was on the phone I'd noticed a slight French accent, so I answered him in French: "I can understand how frustrated you must be, but I just want to call Customs and then you can have the phone again."

After my call I passed by his boat, a Columbia 45-footer named *Dramis*. The boat had a center cockpit over a flush deck, and she looked very roomy and comfortable. The owner was on deck talking with a friend and called me over to ask where I'd come in from. I answered him and asked, "What type of transmission do you have? Do you know what the problem is?"

"The engine is a Perkins 4-108," he replied. "The transmission I'm not sure of, but we have to refill the oil every hour and I don't want to chance going too far."

"I used to work in a boatyard in Fort Lauderdale," I said. "Mind if I look at it after I'm cleared in?"

"That would be super. We've lost three days so far and I have disappointed guests on board."

By late that afternoon I was on his boat with my tool bag, opening hatches in the main salon to reach the engine. I located the problem, and by 7 p.m., the repairs were done. He insisted I join his party for dinner on shore. I accepted and we introduced ourselves. His name was Jean Simard (the boat's name spelled backward), and he told me he went sailing for one week every month. I learned that he and his brothers were owners and directors of Marine Industry, Ltd., an old shipbuilding company based in Sorel, Quebec. Three of the four brothers were boat enthusiasts.

During dinner, Jean and his guests talked about resuming their trip the next day. The guests had flights back to Canada on Sunday night; after the loss of three days, there simply wasn't enough time to sail to the Bahamas and back. Wanting to help again, I said, "May I make a suggestion? Maybe you could have your guests fly home from Freeport on Sunday, and I could fly in Monday to help you bring the boat back to Miami on Monday or Tuesday." They liked the idea and said, "After all you did for us, you would do that?"

I replied, "Hold on there. Helping you this afternoon was one thing, but going to Freeport and helping you bring the boat back is another matter. I am a licensed captain and I would need to charge a fee, plus air fare and expenses."

"No problem," Jean said. "But can I depend on you to be there?"

"I did get your boat going this afternoon," I said, "and I'll make sure she comes back to Miami safely. That's what I do."

I flew in to the Bahamas on the Monday. Jean had prepared everything and was waiting for me to cast off. On the way to Miami, we got to know more about each other. We discovered we had both participated in swimming competitions—and at the same pool! I competed in swimming and diving eight years after he did, and we knew the same coaches and club members. After this discovery, every morning before our first coffee we'd swim a couple of circles around the boat. We'd grab a hold of the anchor chain afterward, and there we would plan the rest of the day.

Jean paid me upon our arrival in Miami and said, "My older brother Arthur and a couple of his friends are coming to the boat in three weeks. He's not much on sailing—he's a powerboat man—and I could use some help if you're available."

On this second trip, we sailed into Lyford Cay Marina, on the west end of New Providence, Bahamas. While we were docking, someone dropped the boat hook overboard; after we secured the boat, I grabbed a face mask to dive the 12 feet below and retrieve it. Under the boat, I saw large broken concrete slabs, apparently from some old dock that had caved in years ago. Then I spotted at least 10 lobsters sitting in a row under a ledge, with their antennae sticking out. I quickly found the lost boat hook and returned it to the deck, then got the spear gun from the cockpit locker and swam back down to the ledge. I returned with two lobsters, then moved to the companionway and shouted at the guests below, "Hey, take a look! I got lunch for today!"

Jean said, "Holy smoke! Where did you get those?"

"Under the boat," I said, with a big grin. "They were waiting for me."

When they returned home, Jean told the story to everyone in Sorel, but no one wanted to believe him. But please believe me, it really did happen!

At the end of the week, Arthur Simard asked me if I would run his powerboat to Lake Ontario via the Rideau Canal that summer. As the eldest sibling, Arthur felt a great weight and responsibility on his shoulders. Unlike his athletic younger brothers, he was quiet, serious. Not often, but on certain days, I found him warm and energetic; he had a smile that was contagious and could light up the whole room. I felt like I'd do anything for him, just to see that beautiful smile.

I really preferred doing deliveries—and spending my free time on my latest boat, the 35-foot sloop *Mal de Terre*—but this was too good to pass up. For the next two summers I skippered the Simard family's spectacular 66-foot antique wooden boat, the *Dolphin*. She was built in 1927 by the Consolidated Boats Company in Long Island, New York, and to this day, the Simards are still her original owners. The interior paneling, furniture, and fixtures were all original— everything but the engines and a few electronics upgrades for the owners' comfort and safety. Her black hull and varnished mahogany superstructure made her a favorite at the Classic Boat Week in the Thousand Islands. From 1972 to 1975, I also moved Mr. Jean Simard's boat *Dramis* back and forth between Miami and Canada each spring and fall.

Then, in early May of 1983, I agreed to sail Leon Simard's 50-foot Hinckley yawl from Maine to the Caribbean and stay with the boat for the winter season. Leon was the second oldest of the Simard brothers, a soft-spoken man, extremely energetic, with piercing blue eyes and a mischievous grin. He had been sailing for the better part of his life, and his passion for detail was infinite. When he first set eyes on the yawl five years earlier at the Hinckley Boat Company in Maine, the builders were putting final touches to the beautiful dark blue hull, getting the boat ready for the Annapolis Boat Show. He purchased the boat that same day, but had to wait six weeks before taking possession after the show. He named her *Blue Onyx* and, when the show was over, he and a delivery captain from Hinckley sailed her to Miami. The *Blue Onyx* (pictured on the front cover) is a beautiful boat, and exciting to sail. She can really carry her sails; she's well-balanced and easy on the helm, almost like sailing a big dinghy. Later that year, Leon sailed the boat to the Mediterranean with a hired captain and crew, returning to Maine in the summer of 1982.

Leon and I had sailed together before on the *Dramis* in the Bahamas, and I knew what was expected of me. He was a very knowledgeable sailor, and worked as hard as I did sailing to all the wonderful places he wanted to see. We shared all the work of manning the boat and shared all the fun as well. We developed a close relationship that endures to this day, and we still visit each other regularly. I became a full-time employee of the family. I was so busy sailing and taking care of their vessels, I had little time for my own boat. Whenever I had a chance I would take her out for a sail solo, and sometimes I'd get members of my crew to join me. Jerry, one of my crew, said, "You're like a postman that goes out for a walk on his day off!"

I told him, "I can't complain. I get to sail on larger and more comfortable yachts all over the place with friendly people, and I get paid to do exactly what I like to be doing. Meanwhile, I worry all the time and think about this little boat. She has no refrigeration, air conditioning, electric pumps or electronics. But she's mine, and this is where I come to relax and spend time with my friends."

We sailed the coast of Maine to the Cape Cod Canal on the *Blue Onyx* and entered Newport Harbor on a calm morning. Leon maneuvered between boats in the crowded harbor at the Ida Lewis Yacht Club, trying to find the mooring he'd reserved and paid for 12 months earlier. He'd known very well it would be impossible to find any accommodations this time of year, especially with the America's Cup trials taking place and the finals soon approaching. We were searching for our reserved spot, which would be marked by a floating yellow ball with the number 18. As we slid slowly between boats, we stared at the array of spectacular vessels, checking their names and ports of call and occasionally recognizing a boat we had seen before in other places. All the while, the yacht club launches were busily ferrying people from the shore to the moored boats.

An hour later, we were still looking for the elusive mooring, while marveling at the sleek mega yachts, and the numerous retired 12-meter boats pulling on their moorings. One of our guests said, "This is fun; I don't mind doing this all day!" With the help of the club's launch's captain, our assigned spot was finally located. We quickly attached our named flag on a whip to mooring 18 and claimed it as our private mooring for the duration of the races.

The harbor was overflowing with visiting yachts, and ashore the streets were crowded with crew members and tourists. Every restaurant had a waiting line, and the bars were busy with rambunctious sailors doing what they do best. We took part in the festivities, but mostly stayed close to the boat to join the parade of spectator boats at the starting line every racing day.

Our biggest challenge each day was jockeying between fellow spectators for a spot near the committee boat, to get a glimpse of the racing boats scrambling for an advantageous position at the starting line, and waiting for the starting gun. This was a sport in itself, because whenever we found a favorable viewing spot, the official harbor police boat would order us to move back or away, and we'd have to start all over and find a new spot.

With so many boats surrounding us, we'd patiently weave our way back in as much as we dared in order to be near the front of the line again. In a way, we were part of the festivities, but also part of the problem. The faster motorboats would follow the race to the next buoy, while we stayed near the committee boat to keep our turf at the finish line and listen to the radio for commentary on the race. Spectators ashore had it easier if they had access to closed circuit TV or simply waited for the evening broadcast news to give the highlights of the race. Apart from the race itself, the most exciting and amusing part of each day came at its end, when over a thousand boats would return to port at the same time and create a bottleneck near the harbor entrance—better known as the "Collision Circuit." With no room to maneuver and everyone completely stopped, none of us could prevent our boats' fenders from marking up the brand new paint jobs around us.

The situation was hilarious. Chatting and saluting everyone on the boats closest to us, we made the best of it. Some crew members even stepped from boat to boat with drinks in hand, ensuring the evening's celebrations got under way. Eventually, we'd all move forward to our respective moorings, sometimes missing a crew member or having acquired a few strangers from another boat—believe me, we met a lot of interesting people that way.

We'd have dinner aboard the *Blue Onyx* most evenings and join the overlapping parties in the harbor later at night. What a great time to be in Newport!

Finally, after two weeks of competitors squabbling over the many regulations imposed by the New York Yacht Club (NYYC), talks of illegal measurements and types of wing keels (the infamous "Keelgate"), with a mountain of intricate rules only a bunch of lawyers could translate, the action that took place on the race course itself prevailed. The surprising victory for the Australians shocked everyone. For the first time in 137 years, a challenger had succeeded in taking away the America's Cup from the NYYC.

For John Bertram, the winning skipper of the *Australia II*, the trophy would be transferred from the NYYC to the Fremantle Yacht Club; from then on, the conquering Australians would have center stage. Celebrations took place in the sailing community all over the world, revealing how boaters felt about the past management of the Cup. The victory would change the way the America's Cup would be handled in the years ahead.

We supported and cheered the crew of *Australia II* during the races and shared in their excitement and celebrations afterward. At a party two days after the big victory, Sir Allen Bond, sponsor and owner of the *Australia II*, made an after-dinner speech, congratulating the crew and support team and thanking them for the fantastic job they had done, as well as the many friends who had cheered for them all summer, and all the fans for their presence. As a final note, he said, "I want to invite everyone here tonight to come to Australia for the next challenge that will be held in Fremantle in 1987 and BYOB—Bring Your Own Boat!" With that, the room erupted into tremendous and raucous cheers. The party had just begun.

We finally made it back to our boat sometime before dawn, laughing and weaving all the way. I didn't think much more about Mr. Bond's remark until Leon said, "Sailing to Australia... that would make a nice cruise." He started making inquiries: How many miles was it? What route would we take? How long would it take to sail there? It soon became evident that he had taken Sir Bond's invitation seriously! I was overwhelmed just thinking about sailing to Fremantle. Whether you took the eastward or the westward route, it was as far as you could get from these waters.

We headed south on the *Blue Onyx* and had a successful tour of the Caribbean, taking on passengers and crew at different ports. I loved this boat more than any other I had ever sailed before. I took great pride in her appearance and made every effort to keep her in top condition. When Mrs. Simard came aboard, she asked her husband, "Why can't I smoke on the boat?"

"The Captain does not allow anyone to smoke below," Leon replied. "He installed two ashtrays in the cockpit— that's the only place you can smoke. And no wearing street shoes or messing up the order that the magazines and books on the navigation table are displayed; he has a fit when things are a mess. He insisted on doing the varnishing himself and he's always fussing over everything. You know, we're often away from our boat, and I'm glad to have someone like him who takes such personal interest in it."

In the spring of 1985 I stored the *Blue Onyx* at a marina in Florida while I delivered the *Dramis* from Miami to Canada for Jean. When I returned, I found Leon with two associates on board the *Blue Onyx* waiting for me. "We are going to participate in the Daytona Beach to Bermuda race," Leon said, "and we want you to prepare the boat for racing."

My nephew Michel was nearby at the time, and I asked him to join us. I told this little crew: "What I can do is help you get ready and make sure you are familiar with all the gear and systems on the boat. When you're racing, the pressure to perform is on 24 hours a day. The sail changes are more frequent, and we'll have much less leisure time to rest if we want to do well in this race. It will be the four of you who are going to lose or win this race." They all nodded their heads in agreement. "I don't want to sound antisocial," I went on, "but it's difficult to be with friends who are out here for a holiday rather than to race seriously. We need to stop the late-night socializing, and I strongly suggest that we start training immediately for the few remaining days before the race. We'll have our party later, at the St. George Yacht Club in Bermuda."

We began each day early with yoga exercises for everyone, followed by sailing offshore to get them familiar with the location of the safety equipment, the rules for wearing safety harnesses, and a few starting tactics. We also had MOB (Man Overboard) practices. The first one was a disaster, but the second time around they knew what was expected and did very well. We practiced tacking in the kind of rough water we'd be racing in and did a few spinnaker runs. Reefing the mainsail in and taking the reefs out a few times, we also made head sail changes, then went back into the harbor to break for lunch. Every day after lunch, we'd check all the equipment and fittings; it was unlikely that we'd find anything wrong, but doing this was essential for peace of mind.

I told them, "It's important that you know the other man's job. All working tasks must be interchangeable and executed by whoever is on watch at the time." Surprisingly, they all enjoyed the training and felt they were part of an elite group. In the close confines of the boat, the "Mr. Simard"s and other forms of formal address were dropped and we all started using first names. Leon made everyone feel at home and was very generous with his praise.

The day of the race finally came. We did well on the starting line; Leon was fearless about maneuvering around the other boats in his way, getting to the starting line for the gun. Our crew stayed alert and sailed the boat efficiently. We managed to find little advantages here and there and passed a few rivals early in the race. Leon did more than his share of the work as always.

The next day we had a hairy downwind rush during a squall. We surfed down one wave holding 13 knots for about 20 seconds, and Leon grumbled when I called for a reef. The crew worked harder than I expected, and they were swept into a world of excitement as we carried full mizzen staysail and spinnaker for nearly 30 hours.

We were the first in our class to cross the finish line and earned second place; the 44-foot *Carla*, a wishbone ketch, won first place on corrected time. The celebrations at the St. George Yacht Club afterward were a lot of fun, as I recall. It was my fourth time at the SGYC, and I introduced the crew to the Dark and Stormy, a popular local drink.

After the race, Leon resumed our discussion about sailing to Australia. We got busy planning for the possibility and looking at all the lists we had accumulated so far for the things we needed to do. Leon finally said, "It's time to go to the boatyard." The dream was about to become a reality.

THE EARLY YEARS

Little did I know when I was a child that some day I would be captaining yachts and boats all over the world. I was born in 1926 on the Bay des Chaleurs, New Brunswick, near the sea, but my family moved to Montreal when I was three, before I could develop my love for the water. We—my parents, me, and my seven siblings—lived in a three-bedroom, cold water flat. The three oldest children went to work because my father was unable to find a job. At the age of 12, I left school to help support the family, delivering groceries on a bicycle.

The Saint Louis Bath House was near our home, and every Friday and Saturday, everyone went there to clean up. For a nickel you got a towel, a small soap, and the use of the pool and showers. For us kids, the pool was like a trip to the beach. It was at that pool that I discovered I felt truly at home in the water. I was a happy child. I had a new bike and a fun job where I charmed the customers to make more tips. And although I gave my mother most of the money I earned, I kept back a few tips, which I used to frequent the pool every day. Then I discovered that by joining the swim team I could get in for free. By the end of the year I was competing in swimming and diving competitions. In 1945 I joined a diving act with the Neal Bros Circus, and we toured the Maritime provinces. In the act I dived from 90 feet high into a small tank of water. Eventually I became the featured attraction with Buster Crabbe's Aqua Parade. We worked in Chicago, Los Angeles, Las Vegas, and in Blackpool, England, for the Water Follies.

After eight years of professional diving I had a terrible accident and fractured a leg. The doctors did a fusion on my ankle and that ended all possibilities of ever diving again. Running and playing tennis were also out of reach. That ended my colorful career. I spent a year on crutches and struggled for several more years in misery and despair.

While I was temporarily working as a pool attendant at a resort hotel, I was introduced to sailing by a friend and discovered I could do this with ease. I quickly signed on as crew on weekend racing boats and I liked that a lot. I was so happy to find something I could do that, before long, I had purchased a 27-foot wooden sloop and pointed the bow toward the south. I had no idea how far I was going or where. This turn of events reminded me again how powerful strong desires can be. If you believe, you are capable of more than you ever imagined.

In Sept. 1962, I was sailing down the Chesapeake Bay on *Diver*. I had named the boat in memory of my previous occupation and my newfound passion for scuba diving and sailing. She was a modest little boat with a port and starboard bunk and a small table that folded up against the bulkhead. Forward there was a head, a little sink and storage. Near the companionway there was a two-burner kerosene stove and a small icebox I used as a storage locker—I never did put any ice in it. There were two large lockers for storage in the small cockpit, and the 9 HP Johnson outboard made her easy to handle under sail or power. I was having a grand old time learning about the cruising life and wondering what the next challenge would be. I dropped anchor in front of the Portsmouth Naval Hospital near marker #1 of the Intracoastal Waterway, a sheltered passage for boats that runs the length of the US Atlantic coast.

I was getting ready for a good night's rest when out of the darkness I heard someone shout, "You're mighty close to my boat!"

Looking past the end of my own boat, I saw the bowsprit of another boat three meters away. I shouted to the man on the foredeck, "I paid out too much anchor line; I'll go forward and pull some in!"

I took back 10 meters of anchor line and returned to the cockpit. I heard the other boat releasing more chain. I sat down with my back resting on the cabin side and began admiring the view of the city of Norfolk across the river. I looked back occasionally at the other boats nearby, making sure I had taken in enough line.

Early the next morning the man from the night before was in his dinghy alongside my boat. He wanted to know if I had a weather report. "I have an RDF radio with two weather channels," I told him.

"Sorry about last night," I said, as I invited him aboard.

"No problem," he replied. "I was just concerned for my boat, until you shortened the line."

Over coffee and peanut butter sandwiches, I learned his name was Fred Speary. Fred had sailed from Rochester, NY, where in his younger days he had helped his father build a boat and sailed with him for years on Lake Ontario. Later he'd purchased his 30-foot boat, a Collin Archer design; he'd rebuilt it almost entirely in the past two years, while working at a boatyard as a ship's carpenter.

Fred's boat had a dark green hull, and a light yellow trim on the hatches and toe rail; there were baggy wrinkles on the shrouds and a spectacular carved eagle on the transom. Below the boat's name, *Prowler*, he had carved in smaller script: "He who goes to sea for pleasure, will go to hell for a pastime."

The boat had character and looked well cared for. "I plan to reach Miami or bust," Fred told me. He had very wide shoulders and numerous tattoos on both arms from a stint in the US Navy. We listened to the forecast, which predicted heavy rain and strong winds for the day. We decided to stay put and maybe go for a visit ashore later.

After introducing myself, I told him I was new to sailing. Previously, I had sailed mostly dinghies and crewed twice on a racing boat in Montreal. Then I'd purchased my wooden sloop and here I was a month later, heading south. I was using free Texaco marine charts (yes, freely available at any Texaco fuel dock at the time), and I had done what most sailors do at one time or another: I had run out of money.

I told Fred, "I have plenty of food and probably enough money for fuel to get to Florida, but very little for shoreside activities."

"I have plenty of charts covering from here to Florida, Cuba and the Bahamas," he replied. "If we sailed together to the same anchorage every night, you could copy from my charts what you need for the next day's run. I have no radio and I could get the marine weather forecast from you."

Fred invited me on board the *Prowler*, and I was impressed by the beautiful carvings he had made in the main cabin. "I love working with wood, and carving is one of my hobbies," he said.

We talked for hours about sailing to Florida and the possibility of finding work along the way. It rained most of the day, and we never did go ashore to visit. The next morning, we motored to Coinjock, North Carolina, and rafted together in a narrow canal. We shared a meal of beef stew and fruitcake on his boat. Fred unrolled a bunch of charts, and we selected what I needed for the next day.

We sailed across Albemarle Sound, with ideal conditions. Every evening we would share a meal. I learned to play the "What If" game on his Bahamian charts; we would plot courses with parallel rulers and dividers to faraway places with funny-sounding names, finding protected bays where one could anchor to rest and explore. We'd calculate the course and the distance to each destination to estimate the travel time it would take, and write it all down on the chart.

This was our big entertainment every night, and we really enjoyed talking of all the possible voyages we each would make someday. Fred was a very good teacher, and I quickly learned how to use the charts and navigate properly (we call this system "dead reckoning").

At Southport, North Carolina, we decided to sail in the ocean. The forecast was for east winds at 12 mph. We raised all the canvas we could and had a good time chasing one another; however, it became obvious that staying together was not going to work. His boat had a gaff rig mainsail, and I could point closer to the wind with my Bermuda rig sloop, so I circled around and pulled alongside his boat and told him, "This isn't working. I'll head to Charleston as we planned last night and wait for you there."

In Charleston, I waited and waited. I was very concerned about my new friend's delay, but didn't want to alert anyone, because I thought for sure he must have returned to Southport. I was relieved when he showed up the following day. "I entered the Waterway at Georgetown for the night," he told me, and motored inside the rest of the way."

After that, we traveled via the Waterway and stayed together all the way to Fort Lauderdale. We arrived there in late October, 1962. Fred immediately got a job at a boatyard called Summerfield Boat Works. He was a very talented carpenter, and the yard valued his expertise from his first day on the job. Two weeks later, the yard hired me, and we found a dock within walking distance of our boats. We both enjoyed working on the larger boats; the yard was a great place to work and we learned a great deal. I learned how to fix and install electronics—mostly LORAN-C receivers and depth sounders. Together we took celestial navigation courses in the evening. Every other weekend, we'd get together with some co-workers on alternating boats, and the group would chart a course to sail to the Bahamas and practice with the sextant.

After 10 months at the yard, I had saved enough money to sail to the Virgin Islands, equipped with plenty of charts that I'd swapped with other sailors at the yard. It took me seven weeks to get to St. Thomas. When the wind and waves got up to more than I cared for and I wanted to stop awhile, I would dodge into some little bay—just like we had done with the "What If" game, only with more unexpected results.

I found temporary work with a boat charter company in Tortola, BVI. My duties ranged from cleaning, prepping and repairing the various boats in the fleet, to working as a skipper for a charter party that needed the help. That's when I formulated a plan: I would sail back to Florida with the intention of getting a bigger boat to charter myself. That meant I would have to study for a captain's license.

I returned to work at the Summerfield Boat Works while I studied for the next four months. As luck would have it, the very same day I got my captain's license, someone aware of my recent studies asked me if I would bring his 42-foot sloop to Annapolis, Maryland; he had to fly back to

Washington urgently. We checked out the boat together and made the necessary financing arrangements for provisions, crew, and compensation.

The next day, the owner got on the plane, and suddenly I found myself alone in strange surroundings, with many responsibilities. I talked two friends of mine into making the trip with me, and we sailed well offshore to take advantage of the Gulf Stream. With a fresh easterly breeze on the beam, we made good progress on a northerly course. On the third day, the wind increased and shifted northeast; not wanting to push the boat too hard, we entered the Intracoastal Waterway at Cape Fear River before dark and spent the night at the Wrightsville Beach Marina.

The next day, conditions offshore were worse and we continued on the inside route, motoring most of the way to Norfolk and into Chesapeake Bay. At one point we had the misfortune of running into a fish trap structure and spent three hours untangling ourselves; we suffered no damage to the boat, only to our pride.

The remaining distance was a delightful sail. Having a heavier vessel under my feet was fascinating to me and I quickly caught on, comparing the momentum of 18 tons cutting through the water to my four-ton boat. When we docked at Annapolis, the owner was pleased to see his boat had arrived in good condition, after a surprisingly fast passage. He took the crew out for a fine dinner and gave me a generous bonus as well. His name was Walter Cronkite.

When my crew and I returned to Fort Lauderdale, a doctor and his wife were waiting for me with a 40-foot Owens powerboat. They wanted to go to Freeport and Eleuthera in the Bahamas and needed help navigating. "Ask Leo," someone had told him, "he goes there all the time with his sailboat." I jumped at the chance for another trip and stopped by my boat long enough to pick up charts for the area, my passport and a change of clothes.

We set out and crossed the Gulf Stream that night. When we arrived in Freeport, the customs man recognized me from previous visits and teased me about having a bigger boat. We stayed there two days; being familiar with the place, I acted as tour guide. We left Freeport as soon as the sun gave light to the sky the next morning, and motored in flat seas to Governor's Harbor in Eleuthera. I then flew back to Florida, leaving them alone to enjoy and explore the area on their own, with the understanding that I would return to the boat in two weeks for the trip back to Fort Lauderdale.

Life can hand you a turn of events that changes your destiny in a surprising way.

Somehow, by default, I became a professional yacht captain. And I never did charter my own boat. As time went on, I got an amateur radio operator license, taught celestial navigation, and kept busy doing deliveries on a variety of sailboats and power boats along the East Coast and to the Caribbean. I took part in numerous races, such as the Miami–Montego Bay race, the Bermuda race, and the Hong Kong–Manila race, as a navigator or crew member. I developed a talent for fixing anything electrical and became very intimate with diesel engines.

While in Bermuda, I met a solo navigator named Humphrey Barton, a retired marine surveyor from the UK making his eighth Atlantic crossing—four going west and his fourth going east on *Rose Rambler*, a Laurent Gilles–designed 34-foot sloop. I was amazed by his pristine living quarters and the amount of books he had in a small library behind a settee. Barton kept everything so orderly. One thing he said really impressed me: "A gentleman never sails windward. If you plan your route according to the trade winds and the proper seasons, you'll always have the wind at your back."

Barton also told me, "You should call this chap I know in London regarding delivering some boats to the Mediterranean from the UK." He gave me a name and number and told me to mention his name.

Four months later, thanks to Barton, my crew and I were on the Thames River, on a brand new Westerly sloop to deliver to Palma de Mallorca. We made it to Ramsgate the first day and waited until 2 a.m. for the marina to open the floodgate at high tide. We crossed the English Channel comfortably, with a light breeze, and arrived near shore on the other side in a thick fog. We could see nothing, but we knew we were close when we began to hear road traffic on shore and the depth sounder read eight meters. We lowered the sails and motored forward cautiously, looking for any marker to help us identify our position. I could hear waves splashing nearby. I said, "I don't like this. Let's turn back to deep water and wait for this fog to lift."

Suddenly a dinghy emerged from the fog, passing five meters from our boat. Feeling embarrassed, and not wanting the man who was rowing to think I was lost, I hatched a quick plan: "Excuse me," I called out to him, "what town is this?"

"Calais," he replied, pointing westward. "The jetty is 30 meters away." Then, as though he'd misheard me, I quickly said, "No, what *time* is it?"

"7:40," he replied. "Have a good day."

So now we knew where we were, and even where the jetty was, and I'd managed to save face in the bargain! We changed to a westerly course, and within five minutes we could see the jetty and powered safely into the harbor. We lowered the mast and laid it horizontal, high above the deck on wooden braces, so we could pass under the fixed bridges of the Oise and Seine rivers. We passed among motorized barges and *bateaux mouches*, low-profile sightseeing boats that could pass under the fixed bridges in the heart of Paris. We made our way through a network of rivers and canals.

Traveling through the center of France on a boat was spectacular. At the end of each day, we'd dock near a lock or a nearby village to visit little bistros, bakeries and local shops. We befriended a barge captain who invited us aboard his massive barge, with living quarters below that were very impressive and comfortable, almost like a modern apartment on shore. A delightful young woman and her two children were the only crew. He told us about things to watch for while traveling the canals.

When we arrived in Paris, docking facilities were not available; our new friends were already there and said we could tie off alongside their barge. They offered to watch our boat if we wanted to go sightseeing in the city. My only crew was a woman named Carolyn Hutchinson from Fairfield, Connecticut. Carolyn had left her own boat in care of friends in Florida to come on this trip. One day we managed 21 locks; Carolyn was loving every minute of it. She'd counted 196 locks and a two-mile-long tunnel before reaching the Mediterranean. In Arles, we stepped the mast. We had enjoyed the inland trip and were now looking forward to sailing again.

We left immediately for the Balearic Islands. The Gulf of Lions gave us strong winds and a short, steep sea; after four weeks of relatively flat water on the canals, we were both miserable and seasick. The strained voyage ended as we arrived safely at the north end of Mallorca (written as "Majorca" in English). We climbed steep stone stairs to reach a lookout near the Formentor lighthouse, high above the sea. The view was spectacular and worth the effort to get there.

The next day we adjusted the rigging and cleaned the boat for the final leg, and delivered our charge to the boat-yard in Palma de Mallorca. The yard manager was very kind and treated us like family. We talked about the trip in general, and he told us, "We have a boat at our other yard on the mainland that needs transport to America. I can give them a call to confirm, and if you're available, I'll let them know." A short conversation in Spanish ensued, and he came back to us saying, "You need to get there right away, they're waiting for you." We got on a plane to Barcelona and then a bus to Badalona, to the yard 30 kilometers away.

We climbed aboard a brand new 35-foot sloop called *Leila*. The owner and his brother-in-law were onboard. They had taken delivery at the yard two weeks earlier with the intention of sailing her to Reedsville, Virginia, but for whatever reason, they had decided against the trip and were debating whether to ship the sloop over on a cargo vessel or find someone to sail her. I said to the owner, "We should take her on her maiden voyage together and find out what she'll need for a trip across the ocean."

That stirred his interest, as he welcomed a chance to see how his new boat performed. The four of us sailed to the island of Ibiza; a multitude of adjustments and fine-tuning were necessary on this first time out. Everyone enjoyed the trip, and we got a feel for the boat. We stopped long enough to have a meal on shore, then turned around and sailed right back to the yard to begin planning for the trip. I tried to persuade the two to sail with us. They had a little discussion, made some calls to the US and, in the end, chose to fly home after all.

I told the owner, "There's a new gadget called the wind vane that I've been reading about. It attaches to the rear of the boat, and you line it up with the direction of the wind. The movement of the vane activates lower gears that rotate a pendulum rudder and keep the boat on course, day in and day out, automatically. With a thing like that, two people can easily sail the boat, and the vane will soon pay for itself."

He agreed and authorized me to get one, and we went over the list of equipment we had prepared together. We settled on a favorable agreement, with a large cash advance, and they took a plane home the next day.

Now it was up to me to track down a wind vane. I made a call to Blondie Hassler, the man who had written the article I'd read about the wind vane. He had used it to sail to the Azores and back to the UK single-handed. He told me, "I can have one available in three months." I was taken aback. Then I recalled an advertisement in *Yachting World* magazine describing another type of wind vane. I called a Mr. Nick Franklin and asked him if he had wind vanes available. He said, "At the moment we have five of them in the shop, if you care to look at them."

"I'll be at your place tomorrow," I replied, and he gave me directions. When I arrived, there were indeed five Aries Wind Vanes in the workshop in his garage—but none were completed. They were all in different stages of construction; however, in a way that was good, because I could study all the components as he explained at great length how they functioned. "I'll be flying back to Barcelona tonight," I said, "and I could take one with me on the plane, if possible?"

"I'd need a few more days to finish with it before shipping," Mr. Franklin said. I told him, "I need it as soon as possible." I paid him for the unit in cash and he said, "I'll work on it tonight and have it on the plane tomorrow afternoon." I thanked him for understanding my predicament. I returned to Spain to find Carolyn busy getting the boat ready. I did not have to tell her what needed doing; she had already bought the provisions and a pile of additional charts necessary for the trip. We installed the wind vane the day it arrived. We knew the boat well enough from the trip to Ibiza, and we set sail four days after the owner's flight home.

Carolyn was concerned about this new turn of events and the prospect of sailing across the Atlantic. She told me, "I need to get back to my boat in Florida."

"Why don't you sail with me as far as Gibraltar and fly home from there?" I said. "I know I can find a crew in Gibraltar."

We had a long discussion about it that night, and played the "What If" game over the newly acquired charts. She awoke the next morning with her mind made up. "If I go on this trip, I want to go all the way or not at all," she told me. I was delighted that she wanted to share this adventure with me.

We stopped in Motril, in the south of Spain, to visit the Alhambra, a famous Moorish castle in nearby Grenada. When we returned to the boat, there was Humphrey Barton's *Rose Rambler* docked next to the *Leila*. Barton was there, looking curiously at the contraption attached to the transom. When he recognized me, he asked, "Are you following me or am I following you?"

He was about to head out on another Atlantic crossing. I thanked him for setting me up with some business in London and told him the connection had really paid off. I also recommended the wind vane to him and demonstrated how it worked; he immediately wanted one for his boat. I gave him Nick Franklin's address and phone number, and we left for Marbella.

Two weeks later we arrived in Gibraltar. Humphrey Barton was already there, waiting for us to help him install his Aries Wind Vane, which was in a crate on the dock next to his boat. We installed the vane the next day and took a short sail out of the harbor to demonstrate how it worked and make small adjustments.

There were seven other boats in the harbor with us, all bound for the Caribbean. Everyone was looking for and giving advice on crossing the Atlantic—but no one had made the trip before except Humphrey Barton. Needless to say, I hung on his every word. Gibraltar is a good place for provisioning, boat equipment, nautical charts, and duty-free goods, and we stocked up once more. On departure day, we wished Barton a good journey; the next time I saw him was in Cape May, New Jersey, two years later.

Leaving the dock, our anchor chain got tangled with another boat's anchor, and we needed a diver's assistance to free ourselves. By late that afternoon, we watched Gibraltar slip away below the horizon.

This was my first trans-Atlantic delivery. The *Leila* was very comfortable at sea, easy to sail and pretty to look at. Her hull was glued strip planking with a clipper bow and a full keel, and the four-cylinder Mercedes diesel engine made her easy to handle and capable of good speed when becalmed. Her draft was 1 meter 90, and the interior layout was simple and attractive. The wind vane was working perfectly as well, adding to our comfort and pleasure.

On the second day out, the shaft slipped out of the coupling and traveled far enough back to jam the prop against the rudder. Suddenly we had no power and were unable to steer. Crawling into the cockpit locker and reaching behind the engine through a removable panel, I was able to pull the shaft back in and away from the rudder. I quickly attached two metallic hose clamps to the shaft, resting them against the packing gland to keep the shaft from sliding back out. Then I added vise-grip pliers and a pipe wrench to stop the shaft from rotating.

We sailed into the nearest harbor, at El Jadida, Morocco, and we managed to careen the boat by leaning against a sea wall. When the tide ran out, we removed the shaft and I secured a large wooden plug in the shaft tube. I left Carolyn in charge while I went looking for a machine shop to fix the damaged end of the shaft.

By late afternoon I was back with the repaired shaft; however, we would have to wait for the next low tide to remove the plug and replace the shaft. All that trouble because someone had forgotten to drill a pilot hole at the end of the shaft to receive a set screw from the coupling. If the *Leila* had had a shorter keel with a spade rudder, the entire shaft and prop would have fallen into the deep. We managed to connect the shaft back to the coupling without a problem, and sat waiting for the tide to rise again.

From Morocco, we sailed to the Canaries in very light airs, barely making two to four knots. For days, we moved at a snail's pace. After a very pleasant stop at Gomera Island, we finally found good trade winds south of the Islands and were rewarded with three weeks of perfect, steady winds. One could not ask for better conditions, and it was the most fun Carolyn and I ever had. She mastered celestial navigation in no time.

Twenty-three days after leaving Gomera Island, we made landfall in Antigua on November 26th, 1968. I called the owners with the good news that we'd arrived, and asked them if they wanted to join us for the rest of the trip. They said, "We're very pleased with your progress, and we'll join you when you get to Florida."

"We'll be there before the end of the year," I replied proudly.

Sailing downwind from one island to another was sheer luxury for us. I recalled what Humphrey Barton had said about making one's passage in a timely manner. We spent Christmas with friends in Nassau and arrived in Fort Lauderdale on the 28th. We motored up the New River to the Summerfield Boat Yard; I showed Carolyn where I used to work in the yard, and introduced her to Fred Speary and all my former co-workers. I discovered that my good buddy Fred was now general manager of the yard. It was nice to be back with the talented workers who had taught me so many things, remembering the good times we'd shared just six years before.

To an audience of 30, I recounted our trip, describing the big following seas we'd run into north of Puerto Rico. With the boat sliding down steep waves, I had gone below to work out our position from the chart. I was worried about leaving the cockpit for too long a time, afraid of broaching. When I returned to the cockpit, I quickly realized that the wind vane could steer a better course then I could in those conditions. It would steer all day and night; never lose focus, complain, or talk back; never need food or get tired. After my story, many decided they wanted a wind vane for their boats as well.

Robin Lee Graham was also there at the yard, fitting out a brand new 35-foot sloop, the *Dove II*. In 1968, sponsored by *National Geographic* magazine, Robin had sailed away at the age of 16 to become the youngest solo circumnavigator ever at that time. He had had a terrible accident in 1967 and lost his first boat, the *Dove*, near Trinidad. There had been a lot of high-profile coverage in *National Geographic* during the past 14 months about his adventures and misfortune, and the magazine offered him a replacement boat if he would sail back to Trinidad and continue his voyage. He'd decided to accept their offer. After hearing me talk, he also decided to order a wind vane for the *Dove II*. Fred wrote to Nick Franklin and requested two wind vanes "like the one Leo Couturier bought last summer." When Franklin wrote back to Fred, he thanked him for the order and gave him shipping dates; he also told him that Leo Couturier had purchased the first wind vane he'd ever sold. When Fred showed me the letter, I said, "If I had known that, I would not have put so much faith in it." Nevertheless, within a few years, the Aries Wind Vane had become the most popular brand of vane and was standard equipment on many offshore boats.

Three years later, I purchased another Aries Wind Vane to install on a new Cheoy Lee boat at the boatyard in Hong Kong. I was delivering the boat to Miami via Singapore, the Keeling Islands off Australia, Cape Town, and the Caribbean. Once in Miami, the man at the dealership did not want to display the boat with a wind vane attached to it. So I purchased the vane from him at a discounted price and began offering to lease it, as well as other equipment, to clients whose boats were short of gear like life rafts, dinghies, extra sails, and satellite navigation equipment. I would install the gear temporarily to use on all my long-distance deliveries as needed, and now I had a new slogan: "On Time Delivery."

Training the Right Crew

I've learned that finding a crew member is easy most of the time. There are many young men and women among my personal friends, as well as yacht club members, who will happily hop aboard for a few hours or an overnight sail. However, there's always a problem when you ask one of them for a longer period: they all have commitments, obligations, or a need to earn a living, and when asked, they almost always say, "I'd give my right arm to go on a trip like that, but I can't take off for so long."

So, when making a long passage, I take on crew for a portion of the trip only. It's much easier to find someone just for a leg of the trip, as opposed to asking someone to join you for two or three months at a time. An ever-changing crew has a very refreshing and energizing effect on the others aboard, and you hate to see some crew members leave. Sometimes a member will rejoin for another leg of the same trip. They return like old heroes, because by then, they're legends to those onboard. If I really like a particular crew member and want him or her to stay longer, I always try to persuade that person to stay for the next leg.

This method of crew selection doesn't apply to local or offshore racing boats. For racing, you need an experienced crew who can handle the racing gear, and you need to allow plenty of time for training—starting long before the race, and preferably with familiar crew members—in order to create a solid, coordinated team.

For two years I worked on a commercial supply boat with a crew of five, delivering goods and personnel to the oil rigs in the Gulf of Mexico. The work schedule was 24 hours a day, every day, for a 21-day period, then we'd get 10 days off. The crews were hired by the head office and assigned to any of the 18 vessels as needed. Every month when the new work period began, I'd often see some new face who had little or no experience and no familiarity with the equipment we used.

In order to have a safe and effective crew, the first thing I would do was show the new members how to handle the 5/8″ steel mooring cables around the bollards, and the loading procedures we used every day on the boat. I would tell them, "So far this year, this vessel is accident free—let's keep it that way!" I devoted plenty of time to training new crew; I enjoyed teaching them, and the whole crew benefited when they learned from my directions and assignments.

In the late sixties I needed a crew for an extended trip and had difficulty filling a spot. Then I remembered a nephew of mine, Michel Perreault, had expressed a desire to learn about sailing; we'd had many long discussions about it. The problem was his appearance and his demeanor. It bothered me that he had long hair and a goatee at age 20. He didn't seem like a very motivated individual, and he wasn't too athletic. He had no job and like many his age experimented with marijuana.

When I called my sister, she said, "He really could use a different environment. It would do him good to get involved in something. Anything."

I asked to speak to Michel and said to him, "I need a crew for 10 weeks on a 57-foot boat. If you want the job, you'll have to cut your hair to an acceptable length and shave off or trim your beard. And there will be no smoking pot anywhere near the boat."

His first reaction was, "No way! I won't cut my hair." But after more discussion, he reluctantly agreed.

"Your mother will give you money for the plane ticket, and I will pick you up at Kennedy Airport in New York in two days," I told him.

When Michel showed up with his new makeover, I was surprised at what a good-looking young man I was introducing to the owners of the boat. They liked his easygoing manner and welcomed him aboard.

The first thing I taught him was how to tie a line around a cleat and I explained in great detail the functions of spring lines. He was very enthusiastic and quick to learn, and even joined me in my yoga sessions. In a very short time, he became a capable and reliable member of my crew; after that, he was always my first choice whenever I needed someone for a delivery.

In my early years of sailing I wanted blue water experience, and I answered an ad to join a 26-meter gaff rig ketch bound for Australia, with a crew of five on board. There was no pay, just food and a bunk in the fore of the boat. I hopped aboard this vessel, named *Saint Yves*, in Nassau, Bahamas. She was strongly built for use as a tuna fishing boat in Normandy, France, in 1930 and later converted into a private yacht. The only mechanical gear on board was the anchor windlass and an auxiliary engine; everything operated with blocks and tackle, and deadeyes on the shrouds in lieu of turnbuckles. I have to say, it required a lot of hard work, but I was happy to be there for a chance to learn offshore sailing.

We sailed through the chain of Bahamian islands to the windward passage east of Cuba. We had three days of rough weather, and we worked constantly adjusting sheets, changing sails, pumping bilges, and keeping watches at the helm. One day I stopped to look at an open chart on the navigation table, when the French captain saw me and shouted, "Don't touch that!"

"I'm not touching," I said, "I'd just like to see where we are."

Every morning I could see him taking sights with his sextant, and as he laid it down, I would hear "Don't touch that!" in my mind. Not once did he volunteer to explain anything to me, nor to the others; he was always distant from the rest of us. Instead, I learned more about seamanship and life at sea then I ever thought possible from my shipmate Marco, a young sailor from Marseilles with years of experience on boats.

There were many lines secured to a pin rail at the base of the mast, and four of them had tags that read "*Touchez pas*" (Don't touch). One day I finally found out what those four lines were for, but only by climbing aloft and trailing each line to see where they led. Frequently I wondered why the captain didn't communicate with us; I'm sure he had his reasons, but I'm sad to say that I learned very little from this man.

When we arrived in Jamaica two crew members left the boat, leaving us shorthanded, with only the captain and his wife with their two infants, Marco and myself to sail the boat to Panama. I didn't mind the extra work—in fact, I thrived on it. If only that captain had been more friendly and helpful, I probably would have sailed with him all the way to Australia. However, in the end I chose to leave the boat in Panama.

I like to tell that story every time a new crew member comes aboard, and I proceed to give each one a small rope, 4 millimeters by 1 meter, and tell them, "That's yours to keep, to practice making fancy knots."

I ask them all to show me what knots they can do, and together they start—literally—learning the ropes. Every day I encourage them to participate in planning for the next trip, and we play the "What If" game with the local charts. When conditions are favorable in the evening, I point out the various constellations in the sky and we identify some of the major stars and how to use them for direction. They also learn how to identify the running light patterns of other ships at night. Yoga has been a big part of my life, and I have initiated almost everyone who has come aboard; I believe it has benefited them in a positive and healthy way. Sometimes I'll even bring out a book of sea shanties and we'll select a favorite song for everyone to sing.

I'll also introduce them to some of the many nautical books I keep in the small library above the settee. I may suggest one for them to read, because I know we'll be applying a concept from that book in the next few days, and I want to make sure they understand what they've read.

At unexpected times I'll ask one of them, "Let me see the bow line knots (or the splice, or whatever else) I saw you working on this morning." They'll show me, and if they aren't quite there yet, I'll say, "Let's do it again together."

When docked in port, I'll occasionally instruct one of the crew to remove the cover plate of the water pump, and show him how to pull out the impeller to check it for wear (though I know it's not necessary at that moment). Then I ask him to put it back in and replace the cover plate, and check if we have a water flow. At other times, with the boat underway, I'll shock one of the crew by asking him to remove the fuel filter cover while the engine is running. I'll let the engine run dry and stall, then I'll have him purge the air out of the system and restart the engine, making sure that he remembers what tools are required and where they're located. I simply tell them at these times, "When the engine suddenly quits or overheats, having to look in a manual book for guidance is a horrifying experience—but if you're familiar with the problem and have solved it before, it's a piece of cake."

I keep a list of safety equipment, spare parts, and lubricants; the crew needs to know where they are located and how to use them. They are encouraged to make decisions about course changes and trimming sails on their watches. I try not to interfere unless danger is at hand. I like to say, "Let them make mistakes, they're necessary to learning, and be generous with praise when they get it right. If you make it interesting, they'll soak up everything you throw at them." The more they learn what to do and how to do it, the easier my work and responsibilities become.

The truth is, they want to be just like you, the experienced sailor. If you want to teach, remember that "class" has to be fun and challenging for your students. Most youngsters come aboard primarily for adventure, and if they discover they're learning new things as well, they'll want to stay. If you do not make an effort to have a stimulating training program for the crew, then you're just like that French captain I left in Panama, and you will have difficulty keeping good help.

Sharing my experience has always provided me with an enthusiastic and devoted crew. I am thankful for the many fine young men and women who came aboard to help me

> **A Favorite Quote**
>
> Tell them and they will forget; show them and they will remember; involve them in the decision-making and they will understand.

with the deliveries. While nearly every one of them became competent to a degree, I never felt quite as relaxed as when I had Michel holding the wheel or Gilles (more on him later), a childhood friend of Michel who frequently sailed with us, helping me with engine repairs. Those two in particular made me feel very confident, and I definitely could not have done the deliveries without them.

Then there are times when the teacher learns from the crew. In October 1981, I was traveling from Finland to the Caribbean on board the *Midnight Sun* with my nephew Daniel Perreault, Michel's brother. I learned of a sailboat race that was going to run from Casablanca to Guadalupe, and asked if we could join this "Transat des Alizée," which happened to be going the same direction we were. It was a chance to travel with 64 other boats, and I thought it would add both excitement and security to the trip. The race officials accepted our entry, but we needed to add extra safety gear and two more bodies from a pool of available crew who wished to race and were recommended by Touring Club de France, the racing committee. Serge Maddec, aged 20, and Louis Beaulieu, 21, joined us onboard. Serge was France's quarter-tonner champion and he told me, "I want to learn celestial navigation and blue water sailing." He reminded me of myself when I joined the crew of the *Saint Yves*, 18 years before.

We took the lead from the fleet on the first two days. We lost our wind near the Canary Islands and fell behind, but we eventually found the trade winds south of the islands and tried to regain our position in the ranks. Everyone on board had a lot of fun, doing intricate knots with the short rope and playing the "What If" game.

We also had everyone taking morning sun sights with the two sextants we carried. They'd work out the math using the sight reduction tables and the Almanac. Each one would bring me their results and I would check them, and if I found a number of errors, I'd ask them to do it again. Every day, shortly after noon, local time, I would compare what they'd turned in with the sat-nav (satellite navigation) system, which was covered with a towel in the aft cabin. No one was allowed to look at the sat-nav to see the actual noon position until after all their calculations were submitted.

That was the daily activity that the crew appreciated most by at the end of the voyage. All but one became an expert navigator, and the one day I screwed up and miscalculated the sight, they wouldn't let me get away with it!

Whoever was on watch was responsible for the sail changes and course alterations. If the wind piped up, I would come out to the cockpit and sit opposite the helmsman, looking up at the sail frequently. Shortly after, the sails would usually come down. I may have taught Serge celestial navigation and offshore sailing, but I must admit that I learned more from him about setting up and controlling the spinnaker, and making quick, efficient sail changes. Anything he did on the foredeck was meticulously planned and faster than I had ever seen before. In fact, six years later, in 1987, I learned that a Frenchman named Captain Serge Maddec set a transatlantic speed record two years in a row, sailing from France to New York on a 55-foot catamaran named *Jet Service.*

During the Transat des Alizée, anytime I wanted to reduce sail for a passing squall, Serge would scream, "We're in the middle of a race and you want to reef?" I'd reply, "The boat that will win this race is the one that doesn't break any-thing!"

If he'd had his way, we might have won that race; how-ever, we did arrive safely in Guadalupe—in fourth place for our class, no less. And let me add that although we had good weather for the whole passage, many of the 64 contestants suffered torn sails, two were dismasted and one came in with a broken boom.

The French sailor seems to have a win-at-all-costs men-tality, and he tends to do what we call "carrying too much canvas." That is, when the wind increases, cautious mariners will partly roll up the sails to relieve pressure on the rigging, but French sailors are often hesitant to reduce sail for fear it will slow down their speed. We say sailors like this "went to Eric Tabarly's school." Eric is a legend in France. He's had many spectacular racing wins, but has a reputation for breaking more gear than anyone. Then he publicly blames the boat builders or the designers when things come crashing down.

French sailors enjoy enormous amounts of media cover-age and national support, and they benefit from corporate sponsorships. Unfortunately, I do not have any of the above, and I cannot afford to push a boat to its limit, especially when it's not my boat.

I called Michel for an upcoming delivery and learned from my sister that he was off on a camping trip with friends and wasn't available. Then she said, "Diane [Michel's sister, age 19 at the time] is available, and a change of scenery would do her good." I talked to my niece and explained to her as best I could all the work that would be involved in sailing to Guatemala. I knew she had no clue what I was talking about, but she definitely wanted to come.

A few days later Diane showed up, as well as Albert Meier, a friend of mine who wanted the chance to practice the celestial navigation he had learned in one of my classes the month before. The three of us left Fort Lauderdale ahead of a cold front forecasted for later in the day. The conditions were favorable for a fast passage to Cozumel; the wind would be strong behind us, even if that meant a bumpy ride.

I was pleased that Diane liked to steer the boat and surprisingly, she didn't get seasick. I left all the navigating to Albert and reviewed all the sights he had taken only after we arrived in Cozumel. He enjoyed every moment and clearly gained the confidence he needed about his navigation. He left us in Cozumel and returned to Fort Lauderdale, where he owned a restaurant on Sunrise Boulevard and sailed his own boat when he had free time.

Leaving Cozumel, Diane and I threaded our way through the small islands off the coast of Belize, and I began to show her the ropes. I got her to operate the engine throttle as I worked forward, raising or lowering the anchor. Not wanting to shout above the engine noise, I showed her how my crew used hand signals for every command. We'd use the index finger held up above the head for forward gear. Two fingers up above the head meant neutral; three fingers up above the head, reverse; the palm horizontal and waving slowly downward, less power; the thumb pointing and moving upward, more power; a closed fist or crossed forearm, stop, or secured.

By the time we arrived at the town dock in Livingston, Guatemala, I felt confident enough to ask Diane to steer the boat to the dock. She said, "But I've never done anything like that!"

"Go ahead," I said. "There's no reason not to try. You can do this!"

I stood on the cabin top, next to the mast, and directed her to the dock with the hand signals we'd practiced. And very slowly, without any problems, she did a good job docking the boat, all without her knowing the handling characteristics of the boat. She later told me, "I never did look at the dock. I was too busy staring at your hand for signals!"

While we were tying the boat off, I overheard a young man on the dock telling his friend, "Boy! Did you see that little girl bring that big boat in?" I was pleased, because I could tell by the grin on her face that Diane had heard him too. Two months later we returned to Florida, where she met my old friend Fred Speary at the Summerfield Boat Yard. A short time later a romance developed, and one day she asked me if she could move to his boat. Two years later they sailed away together, and Diane became a very accomplished sailor, navigator and active amateur radio operator. After a three-year circumnavigation with Fred, she joined the US Navy and studied meteorology.

Sometimes, I've had to train young crew right on the spot, without any preparation. For example, when Jean Simard sold the *Dramis*, the new owner asked me if he and his 18-year-old son could join me in delivering the 45-foot sloop from Miami to Lake Champlain, New York. He thought it would be a good way for them to get familiar with all the systems on board. I was to prepare the boat, and they would join me in Miami the next Monday.

On Saturday, he called me again to say, "I can't get away for the next two weeks. Would it be okay if my son and three of his young friends acted as crew for the trip? They're very eager to sail the boat north, and it would be a good experience for them."

"It would be interesting to see how well they'll fare," I replied. "I'll expect a lot of hard work from them, and they'll learn plenty, for sure."

The four boys showed up on the Monday afternoon, all teenagers who had never sailed before. I proceeded to show them their quarters and what they needed to know about the head, the galley, and so on. I told them, "We'll need to get you all outfitted with foul weather gear, and we'll add whatever you'd like to the provisions list, so write down the snacks and drinks you prefer."

Apart from the shopping, they had many shorebound activities before we left. They hardly spent any time on the boat during the day or night; they were too busy taking advantage of the excitement Miami has to offer to a teenager. On Wednesday morning I warned them, "Ready or not, this boat leaves 9 a.m. sharp tomorrow morning."

On Thursday morning as we left, I explained to them, "The work has to be shared equally between the four of you, and you will be responsible for sail handling and steering the boat 24/7. I will not do any watches, so I can be available to guide each of you through your duties."

We embarked on our journey with plenty of apprehension. With a good easterly breeze, we did very well for the first two days. The Gulf Stream helped our speed and by the third day, we were near South Carolina.

I was up all hours of the day and night to oversee and assist them in their duties. I was pleased to find that they pulled their weight without complaint—except for galley duty. No one volunteered to cook, nor did they ask for any food. Eventually, I discreetly made up a dozen sandwiches and left them in a secured basket on the table, along with an assortment of fruits, cookies and candy bars. It would all mysteriously disappear, and I'd refill the basket. I did cook one regular meal daily, and served it below on the large table.

Their favorite space during the day was the aft cabin; I could hear them laughing and giggling among themselves. One evening they played a joke on the boy who was on watch. The rest were in the forward cabin, and one of the them would stick his head out of the open forward hatch periodically and make a couple of flashes with a small penlight. The boy on watch, unaware of their antics, would call me to say he saw a flashing light or a buoy to port ahead. During three alarming moments, ten minutes apart, there was total confusion. Nothing on the chart indicated a navigational marker there, and I double-checked over and over again before we suspected something. When I finally realized what was going on, the rest all had a good laugh on the two of us.

The boys were doing very well adjusting to the demands of the boat, and a little humor went a long way. "You guys are doing a great job," I told them. "Your parents will be proud." It was a delightful sail. We'd stayed on the same tack we were on when we left Miami three days earlier, and we only had to reef once during a squall.

Arriving at Morehead City, North Carolina, early in the morning, we entered the Waterway. I wanted to take advantage of the daylight hours, so we didn't stop at Morehead and instead continued on, powering through the Adams Creek Canal in quiet water. The boys found a water cannon on board and, once I showed them how to work it, they aimed at everything in sight until they ran out of balloons.

Our first landfall after leaving Miami was Oriental, North Carolina. We had dinner on shore, and the boys called their parents and girlfriends. When they returned to the boat, for some unknown reason I could tell they were anxious to get home—too much time confined to restricted space and repetitive tasks, I figured. It occurred to me that

I could lose my entire crew at the next port. "Hmm," I said to myself. "If I can make it to Sandy Hook, New Jersey, the entrance to the Hudson River, I could sail up the Hudson by myself—but for the open water off New Jersey and Maryland, I do need their help."

The next morning we got under way early. I didn't intend to stop until we got to Sandy Hook. As we motored in Albemarle Sound, they all sat on deck by the pulpit, with their feet dangling over the side. There were dolphins jumping out of the water and swimming across the bow, and the aquatic show fascinated them. Suddenly I spotted a large powerboat, coming from the opposite direction at a good speed. I thought to warn them and say, "Look out for the wake!" But I waited instead; I wanted to see how the boys would handle it. I didn't even slow down when the other boat passed by, and when we hit its wake, a wall of water shot up 10 feet high and the boys got soaked from head to foot. They pointed at each other and laughed uproariously. It was a warm day and they dried quickly in the midday sun.

We continued north along the Waterway to Norfolk, Virginia, and without stopping, we continued motoring across lower Chesapeake Bay to the ocean and set the sails for a course running parallel to the Maryland coast. The water surface here was far rougher, and we could see many whitecaps. The wind was blowing favorably from the east south-east and we continued on northward.

By the next day, all four were seasick and wishing they were somewhere else. That evening the wind changed to northeast, and conditions got worse. Not wanting to make them even more miserable, we docked at Atlantic City and tied up at a marina. Trying to encourage the boys to hang in there, I congratulated them for having sailed the boat so far and commended them on the great job they had done.

"We'll have a rest here," I told them, "and when the wind changes in a day or two, we can be in New York in 12 hours. From there the rest of the trip will be in the Hudson River, and protected. The rest of the way home should be a breeze."

They didn't buy it. They made some phone calls, and later that afternoon they all climbed aboard a private chartered plane the owner had arranged to take them home. I'd enjoyed having them aboard and they had been a great help. I was sorry I'd been unable to persuade them to finish the voyage. I knew they'd have found it interesting to sail up the Hudson River.

So I called Christine, my wife, in Pennsylvania. I also called my good friend Charles Cooper, a retired US navy captain, living in Dover, Delaware, and the two agreed to join me for the rest of the voyage. They arrived two days later. We were having dinner ashore, and I noticed the wind had returned to southeast.

"If we stay here to enjoy the casinos for too long," I told them, "the wind could shift back to northeast. Then we'd have to wait for it to change again. I suggest we go now."

They agreed. "You're probably saving us a lot of financial strain—we're too near the casino!" Cooper joked. "Let's go."

That evening we motored past the jetties, and the outgoing tide made for steep waves at the inlet. The waters were still rough from the previous blow. When we changed to a northerly course, we had an easy downwind sail. We passed Sandy Hook early the next morning and entered New York Harbor. Christine enjoyed sailing past the Statue of Liberty; it reminded her a time she'd seen it before, when she was seven years of age on a passenger ship heading to Argentina with her parents.

As we passed that fascinating city on our starboard, the impressive buildings shone brightly in the morning sun. The marinas were calling to us to stop for a visit, but we pushed on until we reached quieter waters. We continued on our journey until we arrived at Troy, New York. The man at the marina told us, "The locks to the lake will not be in operation for two more weeks because the spring high-water level."

We left the boat at Hop-A-Nose Marina in Troy and all flew home. Two weeks later the owner and his son joined me to finish the trip. I had already removed the mast to clear the low fix bridges between Troy and Lake Champlain. We entered the first lock of the canal system leading to the lake and motored to a marina in Shelburne, Vermont. We stepped the mast and had two good days of sailing on the lake. I got a kick listening to the boy telling his father where to find the various gear and how to sail the boat. The father said, "That's all he's talked about for the

GETTING ONBOARD EXPERIENCE

The majority of boats are sailed by the owners themselves, with family members and friends. They will often invite guests for a short sail or a cruise. Most owners are members of a yacht club, and many take part in local races and need energetic young crews for rapid sail handling. There are real opportunities here—for beginners or accomplished sailors, those who have sailed with others in the past or those with boats of their own.

If you're interested, getting yourself invited aboard a boat as racing crew should be easy. There's no pay, and sometimes the work is hard, but it's always fun and exciting. Don't be upset if you don't

(Continued on next page)

win—you're learning the ropes as you go. You'll be amazed how one sailing experience leads to another. Should you change your mind and decide to pursue other interests, the experience and skills you'll gain through sailing will always be memorable and valuable, and you invested only your time. I can almost guarantee that you'll have fun and make interesting new friends.

If you enjoy working on boats, the potential for career paths and unique experiences is unlimited. Once you find a job as crew, you should find numerous manuals and technical books related to all the equipment on the boat, which will allow you to study any subject while on the job. There's always a demand for diesel engine mechanics or anyone with electronics skills. If you excel in navigation, plus one of the above skills, chances are you can advance to captain in no time.

There is a French shanty we use to sing in the evenings aboard the Dramis that went like this: "*Avant d'être capitaine, il faut être matelot.*" This translates as "Before becoming captain, you must first become a sailor." I can teach you how to be a good sailor, but the rest is up to you!

last two weeks. He couldn't wait to show me what he had learned!"

"The rest of the old crew are busy with school this week," the son said, "but we already have a lot of sailing planned for this summer." I was gratified to learn that despite their bailing out early on our voyage, the boys' on-the-job training hadn't discouraged them from future sailing adventures!

Lists, More Lists, and Assorted Advice

After the America's Cup Challenge, Mr. Simard kept asking me more questions about sailing to Australia, and I realized that he was serious. So we began to have long discussions about equipment. What needed upgrading or replacing? Was there any other type of gear we should look into? The furling mainsail has given us trouble lately—should we replace it? Should we consider replacing the motor? We both agreed we should.

We had other questions as well, like "What size crew will we need?" and "What route should we take?" We started writing everything down; making lists became an obsession as our excitement escalated. Every time we talked about the project, we added to the lists, and I'd think to myself, "Imagine finding someone who wants to do exactly what you've been dreaming about doing for years. And furthermore, to actually do it—on a boat like the *Blue Onyx*... Wow!"

I remember saying to Leon, "We can make it happen, but we have to prepare accordingly and we need to start now." Looking at large-scale charts became another obsession, and we often played that "What If" game I used to play on Fred's boat years ago. We'd look at all the possible places we could visit along the way if we wanted to, or places we might need to stop for provisioning or emergencies. We'd measure the distances between stops along the way, adding up the miles and writing them down. The chart exercise was good navigation practice, and even our mistakes took

> If you are a boat owner and don't have a captain, then go shopping with another knowledgeable boating friend and benefit from his valuable opinion —and don't forget to bring your lists.

us to wonderful places—if only on paper at that point.

We made shopping lists, a "to do" list, and an action list for when to tackle projects and follow up on inquiries. We carried the lists with us at all times. If we visited the West Marine store or attended a boat show together, I would find a way to call his attention to the outstanding items on the list. Then he would select what he liked and wanted while I made a mental note of what he did not want. I learned to live with those choices—period!

I discovered the rental aspect to this business, and a way to make more money, almost by accident. A 42-foot sloop was sold at a public auction in Miami for less than 30 percent of its original value, and its buyer called me to move the boat to Biloxi, Mississippi. We went to check it out together. The boat was relatively new, built just three years before. The engine and the systems worked well; above deck, there was a mainsail flaked on the boom supported by a cross brace (no mainsheet), three lines to tie the boat to the dock and no other equipment on board. The boat had been confiscated by US Customs four months before. They had stripped everything off the boat for a thorough search, then put nothing back in. When the owner returned to the auction office and asked about the missing gear, the auctioneer said, "I don't know anything about any extra gear, that's how we received the boat. "Look at your auction receipt. All merchandise sales are WHERE IS and AS IS," he said.

The owner told me that he didn't want to buy the needed boat gear in Florida. He claimed he had most of that gear at home, stuff he'd removed from his previous boat before selling it in Biloxi.

"I'm glad you have stuff in Biloxi," I said, "but we need it here, for this trip."

Together we wrote up a list of what was needed for the journey home: an anchor, anchor rode, two headsails, two jib sheets, a mainsail sheet with two double blocks, two snatch blocks for the jib sheets, two life jackets, a horseshoe life ring, an air horn, emergency flares kit, a VHF handheld radio, three fenders, an inflatable dinghy with oars, a propane gas tank, two blankets, dishes, silverware for two, charts, tools, flashlights, binoculars and provisions.

"Don't worry, we can work it out," I assured him. "This is what I propose: I have all of this stuff on my boat in Fort Lauderdale. You can lease the gear from me for $325 a day. When I get to Biloxi, instead of two return airfares, we'll rent a minivan, load up the equipment and I'll drive back to Florida."

We negotiated salaries and expenses for a seven-day trip. "Preparation before departure is what makes the difference in the success of a voyage," I told him. The owner helped us load everything off my boat and onto his and I called my friend Jack Tarshes, who kept his boat at the same marina I kept mine, to help as crew. We crossed Lake Okeechobee to the West Coast of Florida. My headsail did not fit the boat perfectly, but she sailed well enough to make it across the Gulf to Biloxi. We had light winds and motored almost half of the trip, and arrived at his the boat owner's dock on the seventh day.

The owner made us feel very comfortable at his home overnight. We told him how well his boat performed during

Have Gear, Will Travel

When I step on board a strange boat, I make sure to check the charts on hand and the equipment the boat carries, as well as the necessary lubricants, fuel and oil filters. I also have a standing list of what I need to pack for myself: foul weather gear, a safety harness, a portable VHF, GPS, a sleeping bag, flashlights, binoculars, a sunhat, sunscreen, a toiletry kit, a small first aid kit, my glasses and sunglasses, a sweater, a bathing suit and topsider shoes. All that is kept permanently in a duffel bag, so I can grab it quickly. Then I add my tool bag, some clothes, money, credit cards, and passport, and off I go.

the trip, and he was very pleased to hear our many suggestions for refitting his boat. The next day, we helped him install the gear he had on hand that fitted with the new boat. Then he took us to a car rental place nearby to book a van on his credit card and I collected for eight days salary plus eight days of equipment rentals. Jack and I drove back to Florida, put all the gear back on my boat and returned the van at Fort Lauderdale Airport.

Most of you reading this book can probably sail far better than I ever could. I've never won any trophies or medals for sailing, I have never raced with my own boat, but I have crewed on many. I was mostly know as Mr. Fix It. So how did I manage to succeed as a yacht captain, you ask? The answer is people skills, and a dedication to making sure everyone enjoys their day on the water, guests and crew alike. I just went out and sailed on as many boats as I could, because that was what I loved to do most—and I've been well rewarded for it.

However, I barely scratched the surface of the opportunities out there. I had so many demands for deliveries, I started turning the extra work over to Captain Pierre Soucy, one of my former crew. Eventually he took over the business when I retired and returned to Canada.

Boats are constantly being moved to and from boat shows and sea trials for potential buyers, so competent crew should easily find many opportunities in deliveries. Commercial boating and the private yacht industry are constantly looking for people to service their needs and provide professional training courses for crew, deck hands, cooks, servers, engineers and captains. I have listed a few websites below with more than enough information to get anyone started.

www.americanyachtinstitute.com
www.imq.qc.ca
www.seaschool.com (with 94 locations)
www.transpocity.ca
www.yacht-transport.com

There's also Bob Saxon Associates in Florida who are constantly putting crews together for owners of large charter boats. As well, there are many other crew placement agencies whose fees are paid by the boat owners, and not by you. Check out the ones below:

www.insull.com
www.crewfinders.com
www.crewunlimited.com
www.dovaston.com
www.southern.co.uk

Companies in Morgan City, Louisiana are constantly looking for captains and crew for the large fleets of supply boats and crew boats servicing the oil industry in the Gulf of Mexico, delivering materials and personnel to the oil rigs.

If you're cruising in your own boat, there may come a time when you're worried about not having sufficient funds for the journey. There are so many things you can do to supplement the "cruising kitty." In my travels, I have met sailors who do the most unexpected things to sustain themselves. For instance, my friend Walter knows a lot about commercial refrigeration, and in every faraway port he visits with his Tayana 37-foot cutter, he always finds himself helping some restaurant or hotel with their refrigeration problems. Another example is Roseanne, who is a hairdresser back home. She offers an opportunity to women on other cruising boats who want a touch-up or hair coloring at a discounted price and works with her clients sitting on the Lazarette hatch at the end of her boat. John is a solo navigator who gives yoga lessons at local community centers.

Tap and Mary decided to close their outboard repair shop in Puerto Rico. The shop's inventory consisted of 21 new and 19 used outboards, Tap's tools, and thousands of assorted outboard parts. They moved everything into one hull of their 40-foot catamaran and lived in the other hull. They spent four years in the Turks and Caicos Islands where all the local fishermen and cruising yachts came to him for outboard services. My nephew Michel and his partner, Frances, have spent three years teaching English to the employees of the Brothers Company, makers of printers and copiers in Japan, while living on their 30-foot boat. Barry and his wife Beth live on a large trimaran; he sells and distributes Bibles for a publishing company in Colorado and gives amazing lectures and presentations to all denominations of churches throughout the Caribbean islands.

Pierre keeps very busy repairing sails and awnings with his portable sewing machine for sailors who need urgent repairs, for example, before and after the Transat des Alizée Race, which he participated in with his own boat in 1981. Bruce, a dentist from Fort Lauderdale, took a year-long sabbatical. He brought along some of his dentistry tools and supplies on his 29-foot sloop, in case of emergencies, and later worked one day a week to fill a vacancy at a government clinic on Eleuthera Island in the Bahamas. Pablo from Mexico makes attractive jewelry with silver wire and black coral and displays his work at local art shows wherever he lands.

My mechanical abilities have often proved useful. For example, when I left the French boat *Saint Yves* in Panama, the very next day I climbed aboard the *White Squall*, a 60-foot schooner bound for Saint Thomas, Virgin Islands. The owner was helpful and showed me how the systems worked on his boat. He had a problem in the main electrical panel that had bugged him for months, and he was amazed and pleased when I located the problem and had it fixed in a few hours. The boat had a large Gardner diesel engine that didn't miss a beat for the entire voyage.

I quickly discovered there was a demand for services everywhere and I felt confident that I could make a living anywhere in the world that had boaters. Whenever my cruising finances were running low, it never ceased to amaze me how resourceful I became.

Navigating the Boatyard

 Every boat needs a visit to the boatyard sooner or later. You can make it a more pleasant and fruitful experience if you plan properly. Making a list of what you need done is the key. Go over every item on your list with the yard manager, and listen carefully to his plan for how to address each job and any suggestions he may have. Ask how much time the yard will need to do the work, and how much it will cost. Then write out the work order together, based on what you've just discussed, and make sure to get a copy for yourself.

After you leave the boat with the yard, it's a good idea to have the owner or the captain (if it's someone other than yourself) visit the boat frequently, to see the work in progress and help where possible with the selections of materials. If distance does not permit a visit, then you should at least be available for frequent phone or email consultations. Other issues needing attention may surface as the work progresses, and they may need to be added to the work order. Again, discuss these with the yard manager first. Write everything down and give the manager a copy, and keep one for yourself. If you add more items later, repeat the procedure with the manager and add to the work order. But don't expect the boat to be ready by the original completion date you agreed on, and of course, additional charges will apply.

If you have never dealt with the boatyard before, it's a good idea to start with one easy-to-define project and follow it to completion. This can be a test to see if the yard does the work the way you want and for the price you expected. If the project does not go well, or the work is not satisfactory, then you can decide whether to take the boat and your business somewhere else, or change the way you communicate with the yard so you will be satisfied. A bad repair is worse than no repair. If, on the other hand, everything goes well with the first project, you can give them a longer job list. If there is a time limit, be realistic about how many projects can go on at the same time.

If you are looking to buy a pre-owned boat, hiring a professional surveyor is a good idea and a wise investment. A surveyor will provide you with an impartial assessment and a written report of the condition of the vessel. The survey report will help you in your negotiations, and probably save you more money than the cost of the survey. When inspecting a boat yourself, pay special attention to the structural items: the hull, keel, rudder, bulkhead, decks, riggings, and engines. They are the most important and most vulnerable parts.

Don't fret as much about gadgets and less important details like the galley, head, cushions, TV, radio, and the electronics below and above. Depending on your individual tastes and desires, you'll probably want to upgrade some of the obsolete electronics and make cosmetic changes below deck. These sorts of items are easy to change, not too expensive, and definitely not crucial.

However, if there are any defects in the structural category, be warned: they will be difficult to fix, and repairs will be expensive and may be extremely urgent. This category is the backbone and functional part of the boat. If it's in questionable shape in any way, no amount of gadget upgrades or cosmetic improvements will improve the boat's performance, its safety at sea, or its actual value. Again, be warned: even if the price of the boat you're looking at reflects the fact that it has structural issues, you should seriously reconsider and start looking elsewhere for a boat.

After the Bermuda race, we sailed to the Hinckley boatyard in Southwest Harbor, Maine. Most of the employees there come from a shipbuilding family in the area, and they do good work. The Simards and I had had repairs done at this yard previously, and we considered it the best place for the work we wanted done. We told the yard manager about our intention to sail to Australia, and after we discussed the many items on our list with him, he made a few good suggestions. Together we wrote out 26 items on the work order, with a delivery time of four weeks.

The yard workers proceeded to haul out the boat and remove the mast to get started. I took a room at a small motel nearby and stayed with the boat while the work was in progress. I enjoyed visiting the yard, but was determined not to interfere with the workers and careful to keep out of their way. I would spend only an hour or two at the yard every day, and made sure I was available for consultation on selecting materials for the work in progress.

We checked the sheaves and replaced halyards, and we purchased a new mainsail. They painted the mast and the topsides with Awlgrip paint. I asked the service department what the most frequent repairs required on the Onan generator and the Lehman Ford engine were, and what spare parts we should carry. We changed one of the three electric heads to manual mode; if we had an electrical problem, we would have at least one functioning head. The autopilot, wind vane, life raft, RIB dinghy with a 25 HP Johnson outboard: all the above items were checked thoroughly. After we left the yard I personally installed the new marine amateur radio and a second sat-nav for backup. And over a hundred additional charts came aboard.

After four weeks at the yard, the boat looked brand new. Many changes had been made and I was anxious to check out the new gear. Having made friends with the workers over the course of the month, I invited them all to bring their wives or girlfriends for a Saturday morning test sail, followed by a picnic.

Nine workers from the yard and four women showed up that morning, and we had a good sail for a few hours. We complimented and thanked everyone as we tested all the systems and made adjustments here and there. When time came to roll in the mainsail, the motor in the mast under the gooseneck did not function; we were able to override the system with a small winch handle and manually roll the sail in. Back at the dock, we celebrated for the rest of the day with a catered luncheon and plenty to drink.

On Monday I went to office to mention the problem; the manager knew about it and explained that they had the motor armature rewound and put the same motor back in place. I showed him the copy of the work order requesting a new motor, and he agreed to replace it immediately with a new one. That delayed us two more days and we had another short test sail. Mr. Simard was pleased to find everything working as it should and said, "She looks terrific! The yard did an excellent job."

We sailed toward Newport, Rhode Island, with a gleaming new paint job and the confidence that we had done everything possible to get the boat ready.

Time, and Other Practical Matters

 Whether taking people for a day sail or for a longer passage, I always make my guests happiest—and stay in business—by arriving at our destination ahead of schedule. There's nothing that can cause more foul moods than arriving somewhere late. If you do anything enough of the time, it's likely that you'll discover the importance of good scheduling. Always give yourself plenty of time to accomplish your task, and know what to say when someone asks, "How long will it take?"

After some consideration of the question, you may be tempted to say, "Three hours," even though you know that's not enough time. For some unknown reason we always shortchange ourselves, and the amount of work left to be done often exceeds the time we've allowed ourselves to do it.

Learn to say five hours instead—or better yet, six. If the client objects and says, "That's too long," then, as a favor to him or her, agree to do it in four hours. The client will be thankful you agreed to do it so quickly. But more often than not, clients will accept the longer time frame you suggested in the first place, and you will have all the time you need to do the work.

One day I asked one of my crew, "How long would it take for you to wire brush and paint the windlass?" When he guessed about four hours, I told him, "I want you to lay a drop cloth on the deck and use masking tape on the base of the windlass. Wire brush the rust spots, clean it with solvent, then paint it... and I'll give you eight hours to do it."

The next morning he asked me, "How did you know it would take a full day?"

As I mentioned earlier, everyone will shortchange themselves on time when asked.

On board the *Neslein*, a large powerboat belonging to the CEO of a New York corporation, the big question from her owner would always come up while traveling towards our destinations with guests on board: "What time do you think we'll get there, Captain?" I'd know for a fact that there would be heavy traffic on the waterway, or we'd have to wait for a span bridge to open, or there would be bad weather, or a backup at the fuel dock—for sure, something would cause a delay. I made it a habit to always add a couple of hours to the estimated time.

I felt gratified one day when I overheard the owner chatting with one of the guests. He was talking about how they'd take the boat down to Palm Beach, or sometimes to the Florida Keys, and do you know what he said to his friend? "Ever since last spring, with this new captain, we're always ahead of schedule."

After docking the boat at the end of the day, I would discreetly slip him a Post-it note indicating the number of miles we'd covered that day, the time elapsed, and the next day's probable destination. Later on, at the cocktail hour or during dinner, I would enjoy hearing him address his guests and say something like, "Today we have traveled 89.5 miles in 5 hours and 15 minutes—that's an average of 17 knots. Not a bad day's run, and tomorrow we may travel as far as Jacksonville." I could rely on him to do the math with the pocket calculator he always carried. It was our little secret.

When I arrange to have work done on a boat, I always ask whomever I'm dealing with how much time they'll need, as opposed to saying, "I need this by Friday." Most businesspeople will accept whatever you demand, because they want your business and want to avoid confrontation this early in the negotiations—even if they know they have a pile of pending orders ahead of yours. They may have every intention of delivering, but when the Friday comes and the work isn't finished, they will have all kinds of incredible excuses. If they had told you they'd need nine or ten days in the first place, chances are you'd have it in time, because they'd given their word and needed to save face.

If they don't get the work done in the time frame they themselves proposed, then you can make demands and say, "You told me I would have it in 10 days." Chances are, they'll get it done shortly thereafter. Your own commitments to your clients depend on the workers' promises to deliver; allow for plenty of extra time, in case their suppliers are late with materials.

If you're promising to do something in a certain time frame, whether it's only an hour or a project that requires days, don't forget to leave yourself extra time. If you're planning a cruise with a client, suggest visiting fewer places and spending more time enjoying each one. Nothing impresses my clients more then the precise arrival times I quote them. I have no secret talent—I simply add in more time than I expect I'll need.

One morning, Mr. Simard showed me an elaborate brochure he'd had made up with a picture of the *Blue Onyx* on the cover and asked, "What do you think of that?" As I read the name of the various ports on the way to Australia and our scheduled dates of arrival, I quickly realized that the distances between ports weren't accurate and the dates listed were completely unrealistic. I said, "I wish you had consulted me before going to the printer with this."

"I have important meetings on certain dates," he replied, "and I need to make travel arrangements."

"Then with your permission, I'll make a new schedule, taking into consideration the dates you need to travel and the probable itinerary for the actual distances."

A few days later I submitted my revised schedule for his approval. He slowly read what I presented and agreed to print another brochure. I knew that now he would hold me to everything I'd written, but I knew I'd allowed enough time for each leg of the trip. To everyone's amazement and delight, after seven months of traveling on a sailboat across the Pacific and the Indian Ocean, we arrived in Fremantle, Australia, on August 30th—two days ahead of the predicted arrival date. And no one complained about the extra time they'd spent in French Polynesia and the Fiji Islands.

No matter what I accomplished as a captain, at base I always considered myself just a man who liked fixing things on boats. When working on any boat, I would often see things like near-empty hydraulic reservoirs and I would fill them with the proper lubricant. I would always show the owners things that had been neglected or overlooked and repair them right away, and I always changed the oil and filters before returning a boat to a client. Preparations and checklists before departure made all the difference for successful trips.

A boat delivery can take a few days or a few weeks, and sometimes longer. It can be done solo or with minimal crew, and occasionally, an owner will want to join in for a short while or for the entire trip.

When considering whether to take a delivery job, you must enquire about the condition of the boat, and when it was last used. If the boat has been idle for a long period, insist on a sea trial. You will be surprised at the length of the "to do" list to get a boat ready for an extended passage. You may need to add several days to the total, just to prepare the boat. You must check all systems and safety equipment yourself, regardless of what the owners or yacht brokers have said about the condition of the vessel. It's up to you to judge of the condition of the boat.

Check the ship's papers—are they complete and up-to-date? Check for insurance, if any. Who really owns the boat? If the real owner is unaware that the boat is being moved, you could be considered an accessory to a boat theft! Once in Puerto Rico I was arrested and had to spend a night in jail; it appears the broker in Miami had neglected to wire funds for the sale of the vessel to the New York broker 12 days earlier. When the New York broker heard the boat had left port, he called the police to sort it all out. The law isn't always on your side. What if you are unknowingly transporting illegal drugs? You will be the one held responsible, unfortunately for you.

Is the delivery being done for the yacht broker or the owner? How well do you know the broker? Establish who will pay for the delivery, as well as when and how it will be paid for, and insist on meeting the owner if possible. Negotiate for salaries, provisions and expenses—never give a flat rate for the entire project. Agree on and stick to an exact amount per day, and get an adequate cash advance for fuel and dockage fees at marinas. If you need a mechanic or a sail maker for repairs along the way, you will likely have to contact and instruct them yourself for the work you want done, and they will have to be paid before you'll be able to continue. Don't forget return transportation costs for yourself and your crew.

You may need to add time in order to prepare the boat prior to departure, as well as time for cleanup and securing the boat at the end of the trip—always make sure you return the boat cleaner and in better shape than when you received it. Decide on the number of estimated days for the trip beforehand and allow yourself plenty of time. You don't want to push the boat too hard to meet difficult deadlines; you just want to get there safely and without breaking anything.

Also insist on a written agreement and authorization to transport the boat. You may need to show documents to local authorities or Customs along the way. If you have a mechanical breakdown or experience adverse weather delays, you will have to re-negotiate at the end of the trip for the extra days and expenses. You will need good accounting practices.

On every trip I have to do minor repairs. I keep track of them in the ship's log and add the costs for parts and materials to the final bill. I always write NO CHARGE in bold letters for the labor; the repairs are included in the daily fees.

Always exceed people's expectations rather than simply satisfying their needs, and above all, make sure the owner is happy about the final agreement, even if you're not. You'll want to have good references from all your previous deliveries. More than 80 percent of my deliveries are repeat business, and I move the same boats year after year. In fact, the Simard family was my primary client for 26 years, probably because I loved their boats as much as they did.

On Board and Organized

I fell in love with most of the larger boats I worked on. I would take care of them as if they were my own, making sure they sparkled like jewels. When passengers came on board, I greeted them cordially, as though they were my personal guests. I would put fresh flowers in the guest rooms and dining room. At the beginning I was uneasy about the large expenses for the operation of these boats . Then one day an owner gave me a list of wines he wanted to have on board, and at the liquor store later that day, I paid $2,164 for the 24 bottles he selected. I then understood that my primary function on these boats was to create an atmosphere of elegance for the guests to enjoy, making sure their visit was a pleasant experience. I made sure my crew understood our responsibility and that they enthusiastically organized things to flow smoothly.

When invited guests came aboard for a short affair (two to four hours), I'd select a good caterer to bring an assortment of hors d'oeuvres, and we'd supply the cocktails. If we offered a dinner, I would have the caterer prepare an extravagant meal (since I didn't have to stick to a budget on those yachts) and I'd have them supply a waiter and a maître d' to serve the meal.

If a trip ran two or more days, the crew and I would have to provide the meals, and that was much more challenging. We'd hire a cook and make the food selections according to the owners' requests, if they chose, but most of the time they'd leave it up to us to select and serve appealing meals accompanied by good wines. At dinner time the crew and I had to transform into cooks, dishwashers, maître d's, waiters and entertainers. Sometimes I would even hire a local musical group to entertain and help make the evening even more special.

There are all kinds of aspects of organizing that are less glamorous than entertaining, but are just as important. Here are some to consider:

INVENTORY

The day before we left Florida, I purchased a laptop computer and a book called *Computers for Dummies*, figuring that I'd have enough free time on the trip to learn how to use it. Over the previous two weeks we'd had many frustrating experiences looking for things and not finding them, even though we knew they were on the boat. While waiting for our transit of the Panama Canal, we entered a complete inventory of the boat's contents in an inventory folder on the computer. We took everything from the boat and piled it all on the dock, and with everyone's help, each and every item was counted—jars of marmalade, jars of peanut butter, sugar, coffee, fresh vegetables, cans of vegetables, and so on.

We tried to remember exactly where we stored each item before, or we'd find a new home for it. Each item was assigned a specific location, and to our amazement, everything was done in one day. We now had an exact record of all the supplies; later when someone asked me if we had any more marmalade, I could say, "Hold on!" And with a few keyboard strokes I'd be able to answer, "We have four jars of marmalade and they are on the second shelf in the lower locker in the portside cabin."

I was able to keep tabs of everything coming in and going out, and that made it a snap to make a list to provision at the next port. The same was done for all the charts and books. They were listed by their titles—for instance, typing "Island of Cozumel" gave Chart number 28196 / 27120 Yucatan Channel, Mexico / Search: = under the mattress upper bunk starboard cabin. Other charts were located in a small locker next to the chart table, or under other mattresses.

We did the same with medical supplies. With the help of a medical reference book, we could select from the screen the ailment we were dealing with, and immediately, we were given a choice of remedies applicable to the problem, where to find the needed medication, and how to administer the treatment. We did the same with the spare parts, instruction books and all the many loose bits and pieces one finds on a boat. I also used the computer to write a monthly newsletter that we mailed to Mr. Simard's office for redistribution to friends and family.

WATCHES

We ran a rotating four-hour watch system, so everyone shared equally in the responsibilities on the boat:

Watch A is the watch on duty. Whoever is on watch A is responsible for the operation of the boat, steering the course, making the necessary adjustments to the wind vane, and trimming the sails. If the watch A person needed help with a sail change or some other maneuver, B, the person on standby to relieve A, would usually spend some time in the cockpit to keep A company until the change-over.

Also, before the end of the 1200h to 1600h watch, B has to tidy up all the lines on deck and clean the cockpit area for the social hour watch—1600h to 1800h—with everyone present for the daily meeting, followed, in our case, by yoga on the foredeck. If the boat was too lively, we'd use the cockpit area for the yoga and hang on to the dodger's rail for balance. Some days we even had a cocktail, with a limit of one, and only when conditions were favorable. The cocktail hour only began after we had crossed the equator. If the crew did not feel like doing yoga because of sea conditions, then we automatically canceled the cocktail.

At the end of his watch, A becomes D, the off-duty watch, and is not to be disturbed unless there's an emergency—unless D is the boat's captain, and then he is to be awakened and notified of any ship's presence, lights, weather changes, or communications. No one should hesitate to call him immediately.

The C watch covered the cooking and cleaning for the day. Whoever was on C watch prepared all three meals and did the dishes and all cleaning below, including bagging the sails and prepping the spinnaker. That person also covered the first watch, midnight to 4 a.m., and was exempt from any other watches during that day.

Having a different cook every day created an opportunity for us to share and compare our cooking abilities. For instance, we discovered that Gilles was a vegetarian; we had to accept his style of cooking. He would always surprise us with quiches, well-prepared salads, or something special like Eggplant Parmesan—his creativity was not difficult to swallow. Mr. Simard liked to prepare elaborate European dishes and would required ingredients that we did not have on board, but his famous risottos dishes won everyone's approval. Michel had a great talent for preparing fish or any kind of seafood, even if it came from a can; he was also our most gifted fisherman. For my part, I managed to please them with my varieties of pasta dishes.

Needless to say, when sea conditions were not favorable, regardless of who the cook was that day, the menu became very simple—or non-existent.

We adhered to this schedule for most of the trip; someone might trade a watch with someone else for whatever reason, but we would always revert to the original schedule as soon as possible. Our system had to be altered when the crew got smaller, and we amended the schedule to three hours on, six hours off.

WATER

Water is usually plentiful everywhere, and the 120 gallons we carried on *Blue Onyx* were more than sufficient for a crew of four. You can replenish your supply every place you stop for free, except in some islands in the Caribbean where they frequently have water supply shortages and you may have to pay. But it's not expensive to refill the small water tanks on a yacht. The myth about rationing water is grossly exaggerated. Only when making long passages will you need to keep tabs on the supply remaining in your tanks. Still, it's wise to make an effort to conserve water. Running

Squeaky Clean

One boater we met in the Bahamas was constantly making a big fuss about water conservation. If his wife or guests were using water for brushing their teeth or taking a shower, he would switch off the water pump circuit breaker. It was his way of letting them know he thought they were using too much water for too long a time. He kept this up until the day he found his wife so intent on conserving his precious water that she was spraying the dishes with Windex and wiping them off with paper towels!

Performing at the Fair Grounds 1947, Drummondville, Quebec.

Yacht *St Yves*. Here is where I had my training, 1963 Nassau.

The owners came up for the picture
Carolyn was taking, 1967 Spain.

Careened in Morocco to repair shaft.

Simard's family boat built in 1927. They are the original owners.

The *Dolphin* going through the Rideau Canal locks.

Leo receiving honors at the end of the Bermuda race.

Leo and Michel aboard the *Neslein*.

Proud owner of *Blue Onyx*, Leon Simard.

Blue Onyx at anchor.

Behind the cruise ship in the Panama Canal.

Leon, Leo, Fijean family and Michel visiting on Yaasawa Island.

Michel's pride and joy.

Frances and Michel aboard *Pax*.

Shamrock V during survey, checking the rudder and the six meter draft.

Checking the hull, fastening, and chain plate
behind the guest cabin panelling.

Marcos and crew out for a walk on Park Avenue Boom.

Captain Thomas L. Perry at the helm of *Shamrock V*
in Cowes, 2001.

View of the new deck and winches.

Leo doing head stand on the partially reefed sail on the boom.

Christine and Leo at the helm.

Shamrock V at the America's Cup Jubilee in Cowes, 2001.

out of water in the middle of a shower can be frustrating. And having to lug jerry cans full of water from shore after filling them at a local faucet is not always easy.

THE HEAD

The bath room on a boat is called a head. The first time my wife visited the boat, I started giving her the grand tour of the boat when I was called to the marina office. During my absence she needed to use the bathroom. When she found the head, she just stared at the unfamiliar toilet with no idea how it worked. Needless to say, she was very uncomfortable waiting for my return. Since then, every time new people come aboard, especially women, my wife makes sure they get very detailed instructions for operating the head—then she makes them laugh by telling them about her first experience on board.

UNIFORMS

To gain the respect of some owners who may otherwise treat you as just another member of their staff, you have to look the part. That's why, one day, I showed up in uniform with epaulets, black tie, and captain's hat, and to my surprise the owner liked it. So I've worn a uniform ever since. Of course it doesn't hurt that the ladies seem to like the uniforms also!

GUESTS

As a paid skipper with owner and guests on board, I would ask everyone to participate in the boat's operation and try to get them involved. I would ask a guest, male or female, to raise the sail and if they had never done it before I would show them how to place the halyard shackle on the headboard and have them crank the winch halyard to raise the sail. I would have another guest pulling in the mainsheet and the owner or yet another guest stationed at the wheel, steering the boat.

Over the course of the day I'd keep asking them to do this or that. Some days I did not even touch the wheel; instead I would have everyone take a turn steering the boat. If we had to raise the anchor or lower the dinghy, I would look for a strong-looking lad and ask him to give me a hand. Even if I could handle the task alone and didn't need the help, I would ask for it anyway—and I never had anyone refuse to do a task. Everyone enjoyed and appreciated the activity. I made it a fun day for everyone! The last thing I wanted to see was anyone bored. If I heard "How long before we get there?" or "How much further is it?" then I knew I had failed to keep that person interested.

If given the opportunity, everyone loves to be a part of something and to share in an adventure. I always say to myself, if they have fun today, then they will want to come back every chance they get. I discovered a long time ago that the less physical work I did, the more my guests enjoyed the day—and I'd enjoy it even more.

To my surprise, at the end of the trip, guests would always thank me graciously for being such a good host. That helped perpetuate my love affair with these boats, since I spent more time on them than the owners ever did.

Return to Newport

 We returned to Newport almost two years after the remarkable victory we'd celebrated with our Australian friends. The place was so quiet compared to the last time we'd visited. We stayed six days, visiting friends and entertaining visitors from home on the boat. The *Blue Onyx* looked great after four weeks of work at the Hinckley boatyard.

On our fifth day in the harbor an unexpected storm developed. The waves in the harbor got uncomfortably big, and I had to run out to check the mooring line. Winds were gusting up to 70 kilometers an hour, and the boats in the harbor were straining against their moorings. When I looked up from the line, I noticed that the 25-meter ketch on our right seemed awfully close to us. I didn't remember it being so close before. I called for help, shouting, "We got a problem here!"

"Is the anchor line chaffing?" Leon called back.

"No! I think this boat is dragging her anchor!"

With Leon on the radio trying to reach some help and me shouting into the wind, there was no one in command of the boat and I was concerned about a possible collision. I shouted, "All hands on deck, pronto!"

We got fenders in place on our starboard side, and just in time. The ketch's stern kept coming closer. Everyone was standing on deck with boat hooks in hand, and we used them to push hard against her hull. That shoved us away to port, and the ketch slid by our starboard side. We bumped lightly and she kept moving past our boat. We watched as she ran aground at the far end of the harbor.

It had been a close call, and we were concerned about staying in the harbor. We certainly didn't want to end up in the same situation as the ketch. The waves were huge for inside a harbor, and the motion made being below very uncomfortable; there would be no way to sleep for the rest of the night. It became clear that we were in the wrong end of the harbor, and we decided to cast off our mooring line and try the opposite end. The water there was much calmer, and the large sheds near the shore protected it from the wind. But we had a lot of trouble maneuvering to pick up the new mooring line. After escaping one disaster, we were about to create another. We missed the line twice before finally catching it. Then we settled in for what was left of the night.

At daybreak we checked for damage, and considered ourselves lucky to have only one slightly bent stanchion and no scratches to the new paint job. Our guests were leaving for Montreal that day and after they went ashore, we got curious to find out what happened to the other boat. We got into the dinghy and motored over to have a look and offer help. She was leaning on her side, hard aground, and there was no sign of anyone looking after the boat. We never did see or make contact with the owners of the ketch. I guess they eventually dealt with the problem themselves.

There's a popular saying among sailors: "If you've never been aground, you've never been anywhere."

From Newport, we were heading ultimately for Florida. Leon likes to stay well offshore. He intended for us to sail directly to Norfolk, Virginia, where we would enter the Intracoastal Waterway. Smaller boats generally stick to the more protected route through Long Island Sound and Chesapeake Bay, but he was determined to see for himself how the newly installed systems worked. Leon was hoping for a northerly blow and when the wind arrived, we headed south immediately. We endured rough conditions and the first night was so cold that, with just the two of us on board, we had to change watches every hour. We both looked forward to daybreak and warmer days. The north north-east wind held steady and the heavy seas stayed with us all the way. We carried a reef mainsail, with the genoa reduced to half its size and without a mizzen. The boat was very comfortable; the Woods & Freeman 500 autopilot was doing an amazing job keeping the boat on course, and we tried the wind vane with the same positive results.

We reached Norfolk in record time and entered the sheltered Intracoastal Waterway. We wanted to avoid Cape Hatteras, North Carolina, at this time of year. Leon still recalled his last trip to Florida, when the boat was brand new; in mid-October, off Cape Hatteras he got clobbered by a local depression that gave him an unforgettably worrisome passage. But as a result, he had a greater confidence in the *Blue Onyx*.

Traveling in the canals, we appreciated the quiet surfaces and slower pace, as well as the interesting scenery. By chance we caught up with some old friends, Gene and Tee Woodbury, on their Gulf Star 50 ketch. They were on their way to Man-O-War Cay in the Abacos, an island chain that is part of the Bahamas and where they sail their boat every winter, and they took us to a large seafood restaurant at the very end of the dock in Morehead City. There was a mountain of Chesapeake Bay crabs in the middle of every table. We had big wooden mallets to break away their shells—and even bigger pitchers of beer to wash them down. Unable to talk over the deafening noise, we resorted to using the mallets to communicate in Morse code. That was a fun and memorable dinner ashore.

The morning forecast was for calm seas and a clear day, with east-southeast winds predicted for the afternoon, and we headed out to sea again. We both loved sailing this boat day in and day out, but by 1900 hours the following day, the wind had increased and shifted to south-southeast at 25 miles per hour. Having to tack in this kind of weather, when you're shorthanded, is really not fun. There's a saying that goes like this: "Sailing to windward is twice the distance, three times the time and four times the misery."

For the entire night we had spray off the port bow that went clear over the boat and behind the dodger. Not wanting to stay this course any longer, we reduced sail and set a course for shore. By daybreak, we entered at Fernandina Beach, Florida, and continued on the Intracoastal Waterway again. Using the Waterway may be slower, but it's far more comfortable when conditions offshore are unfavorable. We often have to decide whether to stay at sea for a faster trip or to take the easier and slower inside route.

We stopped in St. Augustine for fuel and a meal. We enjoyed a very interesting walking tour in the historical part of downtown and heard stories of the ghosts said to occupy some of the older buildings. St. Augustine is the oldest city on the East Coast of the US and definitely worth a visit. We then motored south to Cape Canaveral and spent an entire day visiting the Kennedy Space Center, where there is a fascinating museum dealing with the history of space exploration and spacecraft.

From there we took the Cape Canaveral Canal to sail the ocean again. We had excellent weather and remained on the same tack all the way to Lighthouse Point, near

Pompano Beach. We entered the Intracoastal Waterway once again and motored slowly past large condominium complexes, elegant waterfront homes, yellow water taxis full of commuters, and famous restaurants familiar to us from previous seasons.

We pulled into the B dock at the Bahia Mar Marina in Fort Lauderdale. They call this city the Venice of the Americas because it has 300 miles of scenic, navigable waterways including canals, creeks, and rivers. When we reached the city itself I saw a large neon sign on the Commercial Boulevard bridge that read, "Welcome to Fort Lauderdale—the Yachting Capital of the World." And it may well be. This place does more yacht-related business than you can possibly imagine: you'll find boat repair shops, boat accessory shops, yacht-building businesses, yacht brokers, yacht charters, placement agencies for crew, and captains for hire. If you're seriously considering sailing for a living, you really ought to spend some time there and see for yourself the exciting challenges available today. In real life there may be no guarantees, but there are certainly opportunities!

Florida Departure

The Bahia Mar Marina in Fort Lauderdale was a great place to start our voyage to Australia. *Blue Onyx* had festive flags running from the masthead to the deck, and Sid Brooks, the official photographer, took a lot of pictures of guests with the crew on deck and below. On the dock, a parade of close friends were seeing us off. Six of my former co-workers from the yard where I worked 20 years ago turned up and I enjoyed chatting with everyone of them; Fred wished me luck and reminded me that my first boat delivery started right here at this marina. I promised him I would write.

We had intended to leave early but at 13:00 the crew members were still looking to find places to store things that were still being brought aboard. Despite the carnival atmosphere at the dock, at 13:20, Feb. 3rd 1986, we finally cast off the lines. With an unexpected vertical leap over the lifelines, Mr. Simard grabbed the steering wheel and maneuvered the boat with ease behind a row of other nearby yachts; he's a natural boat handler and he made it look so easy. The crew was still scrambling to stow away dock lines and fenders that would not be needed for the next two weeks. Coincidently everyone on board was from Montreal and we were waving like mad at the friends, relatives, and sweethearts we were leaving behind.

On board we had my favorite first mate, my nephew Michel; he had sailed fifteen years along the East coast and the Caribbean and had recently made an impressive trip from Hong Kong to the Caribbean. He was an old salt by now, the most experienced among all the crew I knew, and he was always my first choice for a crew.

Gilles Leonard was with us too. A childhood friend of Michel, he had sailed on his sister's and brother-in-law's 33-foot sloop in Florida and the Bahamas. Gilles is a very resourceful entrepreneur who owns and manages a large warehouse full of antiques, theatrical staging and props that he leases to theaters and the movie industry in Canada. A gifted mechanic who was always welcome on any boat, he was available to sail with us until mid-April. The four of us had sailed together before and knew each other well.

It was hard to believe—Leon and I had been planning for this day for over two years, and that day we were finally on our way. At first I had kept saying it was just another delivery job, but I had become more involved and emotional about this voyage. I wasn't really looking for any wild adventures, but life does throw you some unexpected turns and if you live on the water, the adventures will find you.

As soon as we left the port entrance, Michel and Gilles began rolling out the mainsail, mizzen and genoa. We had a brisk easterly breeze that we figured would make for a fast passage to the Yucatan Channel.

What a relief it was to be underway after the tedious preparations of the last four months! The crew were trimming the sails and the boat was now in sync with the prevailing conditions. We could feel our speed increasing; we cut off the engine and the boat took wing under full sail.

As I wrote in the log the details of our departure, I thought about how this boat was well suited for this kind of voyage. We all had our own little space where we could store personal gear and relax when not on duty. Leon had the port cabin with a large bed and his own private head and shower. Michel and I shared the starboard cabin, where I occupied the upper bunk; we shared a head and shower. Gilles had a private head, although he shared our shower. He had a little corner on the starboard side in the forward cabin, which was divided in the middle by a temporary panel; the port side was full of stores and equipment. The forward part of a boat is always the least comfortable when at sea, but Gilles said he liked his little corner just the way it was. Soon we would get into the routines of living at sea.

Our first night was delightful and we passed by Key West at daybreak; this would be the last US city we would see for a long time. Two days later our position was eight miles abeam Cape San Antonio off the western tip of Cuba. We didn't dare go any closer; we had already spotted two Cuban Navy boats this morning patrolling parallel to us three miles away inshore. The wind was getting lighter as we got in the lee of the island; having to stay well offshore placed us in a four- to five-knots current and we were barely making headway. The entire Caribbean sea pours into the Gulf of Mexico through the Yucatan Channel, making the water level in the Gulf of Mexico one meter higher than in Miami, and that is what creates the volume of water flowing into the Gulf Stream on the US East Coast.

We started the engine and motor sailed to get through the strong current. Shortly after we entered the Caribbean, the reliable trade winds returned, giving us good sailing conditions once again. We passed close to the island of Cozumel and resisted the temptation to go ashore for a visit because we wanted to take advantage of the good sailing weather.

Every morning at 7:45 local time, we tuned in to the Waterway Net on a frequency of 7.268 MHz. The Waterway Net is a group of amateur radio operators who exchange information on boat traffic between Norfolk and the Bahamas and beyond where propagation permits. I was a long-time member of the group and I knew most of the regular callers. From a powerful land-based station in Fort Lauderdale, the net controller (known as "the net" for short) transmits a very detailed weather forecast for Florida, the Bahamas, and the Caribbean. Next, he enquires about any emergency traffic; then he take a roll call of all the "yachts underway" that have filed a float plan with the net. When a boat contacts a station, he asks for its position ("Lat long?" he'll say) followed by the sea and wind conditions at its immediate location; then he will ask if the crew wish to talk to anyone. He will then call the desired contact and transfer both parties to another frequency. Then he will call the next station on the list.

A typical exchange might go like this:

Net Control: "Calling KA4 GUL KA4 GUL! Over."

I reply, "This is KA4 GUL position eight miles west of Cape Antonio, Cuba. Overcast, wind east 10 mph, seas light chop against a strong current, we are motor sailing to get through. Over."

Net Control: "Good morning Leo, WA2 CPX called you earlier, he is on the line. Go to 7291, he will call you. Over."

I answer: "TNX, KA4 GUL going to 7291. Over."

The net control will repeat this process 20 to 30 times or more until he has logged in everyone on his list, then he opens the frequency to general traffic for anyone under way wishing to talk to other stations. He will also help relay messages to boats who have weaker signals and are having difficulty making a connection. Sometimes he will assist in making a phone patch to a land-based telephone. However, as the distance increases, it become more difficult to copy and relay messages on this frequency.

When we got closer to Panama we tuned in to the Pacific net on 12.404 MHz at 2300 h GMT. There are radio nets all around the world, and that is a bonus to sailors, allowing them to gather useful local information and weather reports and keep in contact with other boats or loved ones at home. We received printed weather charts twice a day on the weather fax machine, and for navigation we used a sat-nav, the predecessor to GPS, which did all the necessary calculations to determine our exact position anywhere. Knowing precisely where we were at all times was priceless. The new electronic gadgets were far more accurate and faster than the intricate sextants with their tedious calculations that we'd used in the previous decades; however, we still carried the sextant and we liked using both systems. Whenever the weather was favorable, I used the sextant primarily to compare the two systems and note their differences. Also, I used it to teach crew members who still showed an interest in learning, even if only to prove again and again how efficient and relatively accurate the old method was.

Arriving at a latitude of 21 degrees north, Leon and Gilles spotted the Southern Cross for the first time; generally this constellation is not visible above 22 degrees north. It is a very distinct constellation and easy to find in a clear sky. We also caught our second fish since entering the Caribbean.

Michel had a talent for preparing what we caught from the sea, and we appointed him the fishing master.

The wind steadily increased and we had to shorten sail; the waves were on the beam, making us roll uncomfortably. That was the first rough weather we'd experienced since leaving Florida. For two days it was difficult to get much sleep. By now we were off the coast of Nicaragua and decided to enter a protected bay that we'd spotted on the chart called Serrana Bank. We would take a break and maybe stay overnight to rest. We dropped anchor in the lee of the small island. The calm water was inviting and we all went in for a refreshing dip.

After our swim, a small boat with two soldiers armed with machine guns came to the boat to inquire about our destination; they spoke very good English. We invited them aboard and offered them a beer. They asked for a cigarette, and since only Michel smoked he obliged them. We told them about the weather we had encountered and said we wanted to rest a little before continuing to Panama. They informed us that this island belonged to Colombia and the only inhabitants of the island were a group of nine very young soldiers, aged between 19 and 21. They said, "We are guarding the island against possible invasion from Nicaragua."

They did not invite us to come ashore or to stay at the anchorage. The whole scenario sounded strange, and we did not like the way they flashed those machine guns around. We unanimously changed our minds about staying overnight and told them that we intended to sail away in an hour. Having no desire to spend more time there, we set sail for Panama immediately. Michel said, "The whole scene looks to me more like a drop-off place for drugs."

"You may be right," Leon replied, "and its better we don't know. Let's just get out of here!"

Away from the island the waves were still high but they appeared less threatening than they had that morning. The short break off the boat had worked miracles on the morale of the crew. Suddenly, Gilles remembered that it was St. Valentine's Day, and we were successful in placing phone calls through the marine radio operator on the SSB radio to reach each of our four loved ones. We reassured them of our progress and caught up on news from home. My girlfriend, Christine, told me she would be in Panama on business and that we would probably see her there. We later discovered that the charges for those phone services were $236! We never used that medium again.

The next day we arrived at Colón, the city on the Atlantic side of the Panama Canal. We were directed to the quarantine anchorage area and told to wait there for Customs. It rained the whole day; we tried to rest but the heat below was unbearable with all the hatches closed. Six hours later we got clearance and were told to proceed to the Colón Yacht Club. The customs officer gave us a number to call the canal authorities in the morning to arrange for an officer to measure the boat and set up a date for the canal transit. By then, the total time logged on the engine was 37 hours, with 41 hours on the generator. Time elapsed was 12 days from Florida and we had logged 1,325 miles.

We ventured into the dilapidated town of Colón for refreshments and tried to make friends with the locals, but they did not seem very friendly so we returned to the yacht club and mingled with other boaters. We looked forward to crossing to the Pacific side, and hoped the city of Panama would be more congenial.

The Panama Canal

 Other yachts were waiting at the Colón Yacht Club to cross the canal; we chatted with the crew from each one and found they were heading to places like California, Hawaii, and Polynesia. None were bound for Australia. The following day the canal authorities came aboard to measure the boat for its net and gross tonnage. They would use this information to determine the fee they would charge for the transit. They also wanted to verify that we had the four docking lines necessary to transit (they must each be 36 meters long to reach the line handlers along side of the locks). They confirmed the date and time of our transit—three days from then, at 7 a.m.

Christine, having conveniently arranged a visit to local distributors for the company she worked for, joined us for the canal crossing. Her fluent Spanish was a big help when the local pilot came aboard the morning of our transit with a coffee in hand. His English was limited and Christine translated everything. The pilot was in constant communication with the control center on his portable radio and he directed us toward the first lock for a 7:20 arrival. For the crossing it was compulsory for each yacht to have four line handlers and a helmsman; with Leon at the wheel and Christine acting as the additional line handler, we completed our crew requirement.

Arriving at the large open doors of the lock, we saw there was a big cruise ship already inside the lock. To the passengers way up on the ship's aft deck looking down and waving at us, we must have looked like a little toy boat. Directly behind the ship was a tugboat tied alongside the left wall. Our pilot, talking rapidly on the radio, suddenly told us in Spanish to tie up alongside the tugboat. Christine translated just as rapidly.

The long lines were no longer needed and we quickly scrambled to get short lines and fenders out of the lockers. We tied up alongside the tugboat and adjusted the fenders. Shortly after, the huge doors closed behind us and the lock was slowly flooded, revealing a lot of people milling about on the right side of the lock. To the left, we could see green hills in the distance. When the front doors of the lock opened, the cruise ship began to move, pulled by many lines attached to small locomotives (called "mules") on railroad tracks. The mules followed coordinated instructions from the lockmaster, and the ship slowly moved forward.

Halfway out of the lock, the ship engaged its propeller to keep the momentum going while the towing lines were returned to the ship. The propeller created a strong turbulence behind the ship and, in our narrow cul-de-sac, the agitated water made the tugboat rock like crazy. We were very busy adjusting the fenders to avoid damage. It's a good thing we were still tied up to the tugboat and that it was also still solidly tied to the dock.

That experience brought to mind an incident that had happened the year before—May 1985—in Canada's St. Lawrence Seaway near Montreal. We had watched a beautiful yacht get battered against slimy walls and pushed back against the large closed doors of the lock—a ghastly accident caused by the very same situation we had just witnessed moments ago and for the same reason. These accidents are no surprise! If a boat is not well secured within the walls of the lock, when the boat or boats ahead start moving forward, the wash from their propellers creates considerable turbulence. In the restricted space between the walls, the boats behind cannot maneuver because their rudders are useless when not moving rapidly enough through the water. And you have no room in front of you to maneuver either.

At the next lock we took the same position alongside the tugboat and behind the cruise ship. I instructed my crew that under no circumstances were they to release any lines until they got an OK from me. Gilles asked, "What if the pilot tells us to cast off, like he did earlier?"

I said, "That's precisely why I want you to wait. When he gives the order to release any lines, you look at me first, and if I slowly move my head side to side, you just wait and wait, scratch your nose, pretend you didn't hear him, or look busy coiling the line at your feet. Just wait till I give an OK sign."

As I predicted, the pilot, trying to be efficient, promptly ask us to release the lines as soon as the cruise ship started to move. He became annoyed when the crew did not respond, and finally Christine intervened and talked to him in Spanish. We could tell their conversation was becoming very intense and she had to use some unsavory words. A moment later the tugboat started rocking and we held on to the fender lines till the rocking stopped and the ship was almost out of the lock; only then did we let go our lines—at the same time the tug released his and not before. Then we proceeded to move forward in front of the tug without a problem. After that incident, our pilot remained quiet for the rest of the day.

We motored across Gatun Lake and dropped anchor half a mile from the lock for a 90-minute wait to allow for the vessels going in the opposite direction. We marveled at the variety of traffic going through the lock. Suddenly the pilot instructed us to go quickly to the very front of the empty lock; this time we passed our long lines to the mules on each side. We were followed by a very large Toyota car carrier that filled the lock completely, with fenders bumping against the walls on each side. Its bow towered high above us and stopped within six feet of our mizzen mast. This time the water in the lock dropped to a lower level, and when the giant doors opened, the mules returned the long lines to us and we safely powered away from the car carrier into a river leading to the next lock. Again the pilot directed us to enter first and we proceeded as before without incident.

That made our getaway easy when the large doors opened up to the Pacific side. We retrieved our lines from the mules and dropped off the pilot at a nearby dock as instructed. We then headed to the Balboa Yacht Club in Panama City. Christine worked the next day visiting distributors and was free to join us in the evening for a celebratory dinner. Two days later she returned to Pennsylvania.

During our stay in Panama we attended to a list of minor repairs. Michel fixed a window leak, and because the circulating water pump for the refrigerator was picking up air when we were in heavy seas, Gilles installed a check valve near the water inlet and that cured the problem. We also repaired the electric head in the master cabin and, with everyone working together, the chores were done in a day. Now we had time for sightseeing ashore and checking out the local watering holes. Gilles and Michel were 34 and 32 years of age and normally they'd venture out together for trips ashore. Leon and I are more than two decades their seniors so we usually stuck together during the nocturnal shore excursions. Still, there were times when we returned late enough to find the younger crew already home and fast asleep.

Our stay in Panama was pleasant; we even found time to do a complete inventory of everything on board the boat before provisioning at the duty-free stores, renowned for carrying an incredible selection of the familiar brands that we would not see for a long time after leaving this continent. That was our excuse for stocking up more than usual.

We topped off the fuel and water tanks and refilled the propane tanks. Now we were as ready as we could be. None of us has crossed the Pacific before; it was a big leap and we all wondered what lay ahead of us.

The Pacific

 Motoring away from the Balboa Yacht Club in Panama, I could see a large sailboat half a mile ahead raising sails. We powered alongside and recognized the famous schooner *Bluenose* from Halifax, Nova Scotia. We reach them on the VHF radio and they informed us they were on their way to the Tall Ships Celebration in Vancouver, British Columbia. After looking at our Canadian flag, the young man on the radio, named Dan, asked us if we were also bound for Vancouver. He was surprised when we told him our destination and came out on deck to wave at us. Then he got back on the radio and jokingly said, "Take me with you!" I told him that one of us on our boat was saying the same thing about going on the *Bluenose*. He laughed and said, "I guess you're right, the grass is always greener on the other side." We wished Dan a good voyage to Canada.

About 20 minutes later the destroyer *USS Iowa* appeared heading in the opposite direction. It was so big, we wondered if the canal could handle such a large vessel. We raised all sails and we were making four to five knots on a relatively calm sea with little wind. We were enjoying the easy sailing for a change, and also enjoying having dolphins near the bow of the boat; every day they joined us for an hour or two. In the galley the crew was having a lot of fun. A cooking marathon was taking place, and because of the extra-special grocery shopping that we had done in Panama, everyone was trying to outdo each other to show off their abilities as international chefs.

At 9:20 a.m. on 3 March 1986 we crossed the equator. There is a tradition that when a sailor crosses the equator for the first time, some form of initiation ceremony takes place; we had no idea what this ceremony consisted of, so we improvised. For this special occasion, I dressed up as Father Neptune with a wig and beard made from an unused new mop and a trident made from cut-up cardboard and a boat hook. We blew the horn, rang the bell, and toasted the two neophytes with a glass of champagne. This was followed by a long speech full of nonsense and, when the time was appropriate, we poured two buckets of cold sea water over Leon's and Gilles' heads. Then we handed them each a towel and another glass of champagne; as of that day they belonged to a select group and had earned the right to be called "shellbacks."

The next day we arrived at Port Ayora on the island of San Cristobal (back then, population 3,207) in the Galapagos. This group of islands is situated 900 kilometers west of Ecuador. The islands are so remote that the plant and animal species there have evolved differently from others on the mainland and are unique to this part of the world. Leon had made previous arrangements to get a special permit for us to visit these islands accompanied by an official guide approved by the government. The additional cost was reasonable and a good value. Leon's wife, Jackie, and a lady friend, Clotilde Cappece, had arrived at Port Ayora the day before and spent the night at the lovely Delphine Hotel there wondering where we could be.

The next morning Senior Diego Andrade, our assigned guide, picked up the two ladies and they all stepped aboard the sailboat to visit the islands. Our guide directed us to birds with bright blue webbed feet, oddly enough called bluefooted boobies, and frigate birds that inflated their bright red neck pouches to attract females. In a rocky area we saw a group of oversized iguanas crowded together so tightly that they appeared to be stacked on top of each other, and giant turtles over a hundred years old.

One morning two large sea lions were sitting in the bottom of our dinghy. Michel joined them in the little boat and tried to chase them away, but they would not budge, because they have no fear of humans. He returned to the boat and we raised one end of the dinghy with the davit to an almost vertical position to get them to return to the sea; then we proceeded to clean up the mess they'd left behind.

On Floreana Island we saw the famous postal barrel on the beach; in the old days sailor would leave mail in this barrel to be picked up by homebound passing ships. We addressed letters to Canada and placed them in the barrel for fun, just to see what might happen, but so far no one has acknowledged receiving the letters.

Our guide was excellent and made our visit memorable. When time came for our visitors to leave for the airport, there was no taxi available on the entire island so Diego arrange for us to rent a school bus with a chauffeur for the day. This way we could sightsee, transport the ladies to the airport, and then return to the boat. Six passengers with luggage boarded the bus and traveled on unpaved hilly roads, enjoying great scenery ahead while followed by a large cloud of dust that got sucked in through the open windows. We laughed the entire trip as we closed and reopened windows on our non-air-conditioned bus.

By the time we arrived at the airport two hours later, we were in need of a shower. Luckily they let the ladies board the plane in spite of their appearance. However they got an unexpected greeting when they landed in Quito, as there was a political uprising that day. We found out later that the airport was shut down and their connecting flights were canceled. When the ladies protested, they had a hard time explaining in Spanish who they were and what were they doing there and were detained. I don't know all the details, but somehow they eventually managed to get home.

Meanwhile, we spent the rest of the week visiting more places our friend Diego wanted us to see. On the day of our departure from the Galapagos, we sailed away in light airs that faded early that evening and we motored south to get away from the lee of the islands. Then the calm sea became agitated on the port side and Gilles call out, "Come here quick!" Leon and Michel rushed out of the cabin and their jaws dropped when they saw the size of the whale swimming right alongside of us. The wind picked up a little and we started to sail. The whale kept us company for almost two hours, then suddenly disappeared into the deepest part of the ocean. As we distanced ourselves from the island, the wind increased and we had a steady breeze that stayed with us the following two weeks. I remember thinking, "This is as good as it gets!" This was the kind of sailing that everyone dreams about; the Pacific Ocean was really "pacific"— mild weather, with steady winds and no big waves. On March 16 and 17 we saw Halley's Comet; it was very visible in the clear evening sky. March 21st is the first day of spring up north but where we were it's the first day of fall.

We made our first radio contact with New Zealand on the ham radio, got weather information and were able to make a radio patch to Christine in Pennsylvania. We told her about the Halley's Comet and she said it was not visible in her area. I said to her, "This morning we had flying fishes all over the deck and Michel got busy picking them up. They're very good fried with eggs." She thought that was terrible and not very appetizing. Michel preferred catching a small fish every second day, which was never a problem for him. If he hooked a large fish, he would release it. "Too big," he'd say. "The freezer is almost full with food and I have no intention of freezing fish."

On March 24 we saw a cargo ship three miles away. That was the first ship we'd met in the open ocean since leaving Panama over a month earlier, but we could not read the name and were unable to reach the crew on the radio.

That night we decided to watch a movie, *The Karate Kid*. We carried an assortment of 32 videos, and when conditions were favorable we'd install the small TV/VCR in the cockpit and it was show time. We probably saw each movie at least twice during the voyage.

Early one morning the genoa came crashing down to the deck and partially overboard. We scrambled to pull it out of the water, afraid of tearing it, and managed to lift it above the lifeline to the deck without damage. Michel had to go up the mast to replace the broken halyard and repair the pulley.

By March 31 we were approaching the island of Huku Hiva, part of the Marquesas Islands, which lie about 1,000 miles northeast of Tahiti. We shortened sail and reduced speed; we did not want to arrive before daylight in an unfamiliar port. The wind dropped completely as we approached the island and we motored slowly and dropped anchor in front of some government buildings at 10:20 a.m., hoping one of those buildings would turn out to be the customs house. We had traveled 3,159 miles in 19 days, making a total of 5,397 miles.

At the customs house we discovered that in order for us to clear the boat in French Polynesia, we had to give a deposit of US$1,300 per person to cover the equivalent of a return airline ticket back to the mainland. The customs officials said that they would reimburse the deposit when we left our last port in French Polynesia. Luckily for us we were able to wire-transfer funds to their bank because they did not accept personal checks or credit cards. "I'm very skeptical that we'll ever see that money again," I told Leon.

Heavy rain came pouring down in the evening and everyone ran up on deck for a shower. We collected water from the awning stretched out over the boom; it flowed into a bucket brigade, then to the funnel on the fill pipe of our near empty water tanks. This frantic exercise rewarded us with overflowing tanks and the luxury of long showers.

Leon had intended to fly to Montreal for his company meetings with his brothers, only to find, there were only two flights a week from Huku Hiva to Papeete, from where he could catch an international flight. The next seat available on the small plane out was in 10 days. Not wishing to wait that long, he said, "We'll have to sail to Tahiti right away, and I'll call the airline from the boat when we have an idea of the boat's arrival in Papeete."

So, after a 19-day passage and less than 19 hours in port, we set sail immediately. We threaded our way around the many atolls mostly under power—it's unusual to have such a long stretch with so little wind. Slowly we sailed until one early morning when Michel sighted the tall mountains of Tahiti and Morea, visible from 25 miles away. Leon was able to book a flight for two days later, and that afternoon, we tied up stern to the quay in downtown Papeete.

Ah! Tahiti at last! Everyone dreams about coming to this island someday, but we never believed that it would ever happen. Clearing customs there was no problem. They acknowledged our entry papers from the Marquesas and reassured us that the previous entry procedure was normal and not to worry.

We stepped ashore for a long walk through the narrow streets of Papeete. Stopping for refreshments at a sidewalk café, we admired the attractive girls passing by. We passed beautiful well-stocked boutiques, many jewelry stores, and gift shops; then we found *le marché*, the municipal open air market. Watching the local people going about their daily routines was fascinating and attracted the locals as well as a lot of tourists like us.

The many specialty shops near the market offered women's clothes, T-shirts, pearl jewelry, exotic shells, straw hats, and native art. I bought an exotic shell as a souvenir.

Tahiti was where Gilles had planned to leave the boat and return to Montreal with Leon; he needed to get back to prepare for his season in the theatrical props business. He had done a great job and we knew we would miss him. Leon, however, was planning to return in one week.

So Michel and I stayed with the boat and caught up on maintenance. In the evenings we explored. Two friends, Pam and Andy Wall, stopped by the boat to say hello. They knew we were coming from their radio contact and were anxious to share what they knew of the town. They had arrived a week before us on board the *Kandarik*, a 39-foot Freya design that they had built themselves. Pam is American and Andy was born in Australia. They were traveling with their two children, Samantha, 10, and Jamie, 6; they were on their way to Andy's homeland to introduce his new family to his parents. I had met Pam and Andy 12 years earlier when she worked for Mac Shaw, the sail maker, in Florida; Andy was doing mast and rigging repairs at a local yard. Pam is an active ham radio operator and we have a lot of mutual friends in Florida. We frequently talked on the radio net and she was looking forward to our arrival.

We soon discovered that going ashore for dinner here was out of the question because restaurants and bars were extremely expensive, even though at the market fresh produce was reasonable. Consequently, every other day the crew of the neighboring boats would chip in and we would share a Chinese dinner from a local take-out establishment. The food was excellent and not expensive. The portions were so generous that with an order for four we could easily feed eight. Pam usually organized the group, prompted by her children. They wanted to come to our boat so they could see movies. The chance to see a movie in English in Papeete was unusual and appreciated by this group. After the movies, we enjoyed late-night discussions about cruising and our next destinations.

Pam and Andy visited Australia and later returned to Florida. Pam is now the general manager at the West Marine Store in Fort Lauderdale. She is a frequent speaker and promotes video presentations on the large screen at her store, featuring safety issues or new products; sometime she'll feature a voyage under sail from her large collection. Andy is still very busy with the mast and rigging clientele. Together Pam and Andy have a mountain of experience that they happily share with their customers.

Leon ended up postponing his return date, so Michel and I took advantage of this to visit the island of Morea, just 12 miles away, for a week. There was a tranquility there that was totally different from the first two islands. The snorkeling was very good and we took a bike tour of the island. We returned to Papeete to welcome Mr. and Mrs. Simard, plus a new guest, Mr. André Rousseau, a retired commander of the French navy, then residing in Nice, France. They visited

Papeete for three days and then we returned to Morea for another two days.

With the five of us on board we sailed to Bora Bora. This was the first time Mrs. Simard had made an open ocean passage on the boat and we were pleasantly surprised: she enjoyed the trip but her only complaint was, while sunbathing every day on the cabin top, if the sun happened to go behind the sail and leave her in the shade, she would cry, "Captain, you took my sun away!" So when possible I would alter the course a little to accommodate her. We teased her by saying, "We'll blame you if we arrive at the wrong island!"

The Bora Bora Hotel was a one-of-a-kind experience. The exquisite outdoor patios and the boardwalks leading to spectacular hotel suites on stilts over the water are very special and extravagant. A jewelry store in the hotel lobby had a large black pearl that caught my eye. I went back a second time to look and bought it for Christine.

All in all, those islands are just like postcard pictures. The busy Papeete with its market, and the islands with their tall, rugged mountains and green valleys flowing down to the endless sandy beaches surrounded by coral reefs—they are the most beautiful anywhere.

Mrs. Simard returned to Montreal and the remaining four of us prepared to set sail. André was replacing Gilles on this leg of the trip and Michel showed him the onboard routines and equipment. When we heard news on the radio of a hurricane near the Solomon Islands, with high winds and heavy seas predicted for our area, we quickly moved to a more protected spot that was recommended by a local boatman. In a very small bay surrounded by high hills and good holding ground, we endured heavy rain and winds for two days.

Near departure time we asked the authorities for the refund of the deposit we had made on our arrival in Huku Hiva, and they simply asked us what currency we wanted! We asked for US dollars, the same currency we had given them when we entered Polynesia five weeks earlier, to avoid paying the additional exchange fees that would apply. We presented our papers to the bank manager as instructed, and he said he needed time to collect the US dollars from the other bank. An hour later they handed us our money, most of it in ones, fives, tens, and twentys, plus two one-hundred dollar bills; we gratefully accepted the money, surprised they honored the refund as promised.

Next we stopped at Aitutaki, a small island in the Cook Islands, which are a political dependency of New Zealand. From offshore the channel appeared shallow and we could see sailboats at anchor inside the reef near a beach. We were able to reach one of the boats on VHF radio and they confirmed a maximum depth of 1.80 meters. The person we spoke to said he'd touched bottom going in a few days earlier, so we elected not to go in and anchored in the lee of the reef for the night because we need at least 2 meters.

Early the next morning we got under way; André did a good job in the galley preparing a small tuna we'd caught that morning. He made a sushi appetizer followed by broiled tuna steak. Apart from being a good cook he was also an excellent sailor. I grew to like him enormously, in part because of all the interesting stories he would tell during the long evenings in the cockpit.

Michel, Leon and I were so elated by all the beautiful sailing experiences we'd had for the past two months. When we tried to explain this to André we could not find the right words except to say that so far the trip had been great and that as we ventured farther into the Pacific, things would only get more exotic and exiting. We had no way of knowing what danger lay ahead of us.

After four days of delightful sailing in the direction of Fiji, one morning we could see breaking reefs on the radar way before we got near them. The Fiji Islands are a group of small atolls and large islands. As indicated on the chart, many appeared to be completely submerged. As we approached the reefs we managed to circle them slowly and entered through a difficult pass. Thank goodness it was still daylight. We kept everything on our starboard as we sailed closer and finally dropped anchor in Lautoka Harbor to clear customs. Christine had arrived the day before and left a message to call the hotel. She was relieved to hear my voice when I called.

We had covered 1,840 miles from Bora Bora in 12 days, for a grand total of 8,137 miles. The next day we moved to Malolo Lailai Island, and stayed at a famous resort nicknamed Dick's Place (more on this in the next chapter). I had heard stories about this place way back in Fort Lauderdale, years before this voyage presented itself. I was always dreaming of faraway places but this time, here in the fabled Fiji Islands, I felt I was experiencing more than I'd ever expected.

Staying in Touch

 During our trip, having recently learned to use a laptop and having successfully entered the complete inventory of the ship's provisions, I started writing a monthly newsletter describing the events that had taken place during the previous four weeks and forwarding the letter to Leon's secretary in Montreal. She was kind enough to make copies and forward them to my siblings and a few friends; then Leon wanted it sent to a few friends and his family, and the crew requested the same, for a total of 28 copies. This created a big saving in time, and, mailed from Montreal, these letters required only local postage and were delivered quickly.

I was not aware that the recipients would show the letters to friends or associates and they in turn would request a copy from the secretary. Four months later a frustrated secretary was complaining about the extra work that kept multiplying; she was mailing 86 copies, and some recipients were requesting copies of earlier letters they had missed. When I finally heard about this situation, I simply stopped writing the letters! Here are some of the letters I wrote:

July 2, 1986

Dear friends, relatives and sweethearts,

As ridiculous as this may appear, we had a day with two breakfasts, two lunches and two dinners. (Explanation below.)

When you travel in a westerly direction across the ocean, at every 15 degrees of longitude that you cover, you change the time on the ship's clock (minus one hour). Therefore when we arrived at 180 degrees = minus 12 hours, that is, GMT time.

Your position now has becomes 180 degrees East of Greenwich, and you need to add one hour for each 15 degrees = + 12 hours, advance one day on the calendar. Somehow, we lost one complete day. Confused?? Good, because when we arrived at the International dateline (180 degrees) we had all sorts of discussions on how to apply the change, and to our astonishment, the change was made automatically by our Sat Nav. instrument.

Fiji is a cluster of beautiful nonpolluted islands, with very friendly people.

Throughout Fiji, the drinking of kava is a ceremonial and social custom with a complicated ritual that goes like this:

When invited, you're expected to bring a gift; we asked around for what was an appropriate gift and they suggested a kilo of kava roots would be fine. You place the gift on the floor, if the chief picks it up, you are welcome to join a group of men sitting on the floor around the tanoa—that is the name of the large bowl containing an astringent liquid made from grinding the kava roots.

Dipping a *mbilo*—that is the name of the half-coconut shell used as a cup to dip into the tanoa—the liquid is passed to each person and the man next to me showed us how to proceed properly for this ritual.

When offered the mbilo, you clap your hands once, take the half-filled cup and just before it meet your lips, you say "*Mbula* [Greetings]." You drink it down in one gulp, then slap your right hip once, return the mbilo and say "*Venaka* [Thank you]." Everyone claps their hands three times and passes the refilled mbilo to the next in line and he repeats the same ritual. They continue casual conversation while the mbilo is passed around. When it comes back to you, you are expected to remember the ritual and in the right order. They all laugh ecstatically every time you miss one part, or the proper order. They will demonstrate it again and pass the mbilo to the next man. The more you screw up the routine the more everyone laughs, but you don't mind the ribbing because it's done in a very friendly way and everyone is having such a good time. The taste of this liquid is bland and chalky, it makes your mouth very dry. They said it is a narcotic (very mild); all it did for me was make me thirsty for a lot of water. However, it did keep me awake for 24 hours.

Next day we visited the Yaasawa Islands (part of the island group) for a snorkeling tour. The underwater caves were spectacular and filled with aquatic life. On the fifth day, Leon and André left for Montreal and we moved the boat to the island of Mololo Lailai. There are two resorts on this island.The Plantation Hotel is upscale; it has complete water-sport activities and good music for dancing in the evening. The other is Dick's Place, a low-key resort established in the previous century. Sailors that made it to this remarkable place wanted to leave a mark or a signature of passage; they have covered every wall with yacht club burgees and photographs of yachts with crew. On a shelf near the office there are many guest logbooks, some current and others dating as far back as the early 1900s, with the names of the boats and crew. Reading about the number of boats that sailed through here this year alone, then looking back at the ones that passed through here 5, 40 and 80 years ago, is mind-boggling and impressive.

Michel returned from a trip to Suva, he said it is a vibrant city, with good duty free shopping, where you can haggle with the Indian shopkeepers for the best prices. The nightlife is lively with friendly locals and tourists.

When Leon returned we made preparations for our departure. The gang we befriended at Dick's Place insisted on a celebration to wish the boat a safe passage and they all said, "We know that you'll be back." I must admit that after visiting half a dozen islands in this group, we unanimously voted that this was our most favorite landfall so far.

We sailed away June 25 with only three on board; after the many parties at Dick's Place it's was good to be back to the orderly life on board *Blue Onyx*. Today we have a good wind pushing 32 tons of hull, equipment, stores and humanity, at eight knots, to the next destination. It is this kind of sailing and feeling of freedom that will enable us to endure the isolation from crowds and to leave our loved ones behind. We adapted quickly to having only three on board. We covered remarkable distances the first four days and when I check our position, I told Michel, "We have only 60 miles to Noumea." Then he said, "I'm happy to hear that, but look at the clouds on the horizon and the deep swell that is out of keeping with our wave pattern; there's a storm nearby and she's coming this way."

We both looked at black forbidding clouds rising from the south. "I don't like the looks of this," he said. We began reefing the main and changed the headsail to a smaller jib and within an hour the wind shifted to SW and before long we're taking solid water across the decks, no one cares to stay below, the noise from the waves crashing on both sides of the hull is eerie and we huddle behind the dodger for protection from the wind and spray. By mid-afternoon I said, "We're dashing too fast down those steep waves, we barely can keep her on course, let's reduce the mainsail and change to no. 3 jib [the smallest headsail we have]." We cannot see anything through the Plexiglas panels of the dodger that was awash constantly. Unable to make any forward progress, at 9.00 p.m. we took down the mainsail and heaved-to with a reef mizzen and the small jib aback. It's the first and only time that we found it necessary to heave-to on the entire trip. I crawled in my bunk to wedge myself against the hull and filled the gap to the lee cloth with pillows and attempted to rest.

That's when Leon said, "Boy! IT MUST BE PLAIN HELL ASHORE ON A NIGHT LIKE THIS!"—a phrase we'd heard somewhere before in sailing circles but none of us could recall exactly who'd said it. And we all cracked up laughing! When daylight came we set sail again, got back on course and tried to regain the ground we lost during the night. We pounded into the rough seas for six hours and slowly made our way into Port Goro. We found a protected bay with good anchorage north of the main harbor. Glad to be out of that nasty weather, we put down the two larger anchors. Michel prepared a good meal and we read books while it continued to blow for 30 hours. We discovered our mainsail was badly torn in two places, a 12-foot tear at the luff, five slides were gone and a long diagonal rip near the upper section. Lucky for us we did have the brand new mainsail on board that we purchased in Maine last year.

Leon said, "I'm surprised that we came this far with the old mainsail." When the wind subsided we replaced the mainsail and sailed to Noumea, the capital of New Caledonia (a territory of France) some 30 miles away. When we arrived at the yacht club we heard about the many yachts that were not as fortunate. Eighteen yachts had suffered extensive damage right there at the marina, and a small cargo ship went aground six miles north of the harbor and there was some talk of a sailboat lost in another part of the island.

The Cercle Nautique of New Caledonia is a very hospitable club, and as we chatted with our new neighbors they told us about the havoc that went through the marina and were astonished that we managed to sail in from offshore unscratched. There is a strange atmosphere on this island and we feel uncomfortable to see so many heavily armed military everywhere. I shall tell you about it in the next letter. I am rushing to mail this letter now, otherwise you may wonder what became of us.

Au revoir,

Leo Couturier
Leon Simard
Michel Perreault

August 13, 1986

Dear friends, relatives and sweethearts,

Here is a short letter to let you know we are still afloat and doing well. Our visit to New Caledonia was very interesting; the island is pretty much a solid lump of minerals with a beautiful mountain chain that marches down the center for some 240-odd miles. The island's great wealth lies just below the surface of the mountain tops, it's a case of scratch the surface and you find minerals, mostly nickel and chrome in vast quantities, among other minerals. The drop in world demand for these commodities caused the bottom to fall out of mining and presently they have a faltering economy.

The great distance from France has not stopped Noumea from looking like any small town in France, with its chic bistros, very nice boutiques, French bread made daily, good restaurants, hotels and a Club Med.

We made an excursion of the island in a rented car. Driving on the gravel roads full of potholes was just as rough as our coming here by sea. We drove north to the town of Thio where Melanesian laborers used to work the mines when nickel was king. Now it is a desolate ghost town. Canala, La Foa, Bouloupari are names of towns we visited and we found the locals living in appalling conditions, a very depressing area. What a shame to see a population of 160,000 living in such poverty in a rich country.

Tribal life in the interior goes on much as it always has, blue begonias and bougainvillea clamber over tiny huts with roofs made of layers of white bark. The ancient life in the bush still survives.

With the closing of the mines, the local peasants (Melanesians) have very little possessions and their demands for small plots of land to build shelters for their family and grow things falls on deaf ears. Their needs are real. People have to resort to farming in odd patches near the jungle.

I was told that the French settlers own and control all the land in the mountain area and won't part with any; they do very little farming themselves. Most of the products you find in the stores in Noumea are imported from France or Australia and sold at high prices to the elite living in the city. There's a lot of political unrest here, the confrontations between the French settlers and the Melanesians made a lot of noise in the media in 1985, and four divisions of soldiers were flown in from France to quell a takeover that was taking place in Thio, the mining center. The confrontation lasted one month; over a hundred demonstrators are still in jail and this left everyone here to live in fear. There's a referendum on land disputes going on right now for an extension of franchises for Independence by 1989. The overwhelming amount of heavily armed soldiers made us feel uncomfortable. There are talks of a possible uprising on Bastille Day. We decided to leave two days before that holiday, having no desire to take part in the French celebration or get involve in any uprising.

Michel is taking a break from the boat and going back to Fiji to meet his girlfriend, Frances, who flew in from Vancouver. They will explore the Fiji Islands together and tour New Zealand in a rented camper trailer; then they will join us again in Fremantle.

I hated to see my best crew member leave. We'll need to find a replacement somehow.

We met a young Australian name Graham at the marina who had just completed a two-year contract as a chef at a resort hotel in Noumea and he welcomed the chance to return home on a private yacht. After checking with his former employer, we promptly welcomed him onboard and Leon is looking forward to sampling his gastronomic expertise in the galley. On July 12, we sailed away with very light wind that made for a good initiation to sailing for Graham's first time. We were showing off with the spinnaker and the mizzen stay-sail flying in all their glory; we told him, "We're taking you home in style!"

For the next eight days the winds were so predictable and constant that we lowered the spinnaker only at night as a precaution and to allow the two off-duty crew members to have an uninterrupted rest. Every morning we'd reset the big chute and I heard Leon mumbling out loud, "Give me some wind and I'll give you some miles."

We never know where the time goes. The sun sets at the end of the day and we feel we have achieved a lot; but our new helper is affected by the motion of the boat and those fancy meals we had anticipated from him never did materialize. We did not expect hotel service but we were looking forward to sampling the great food he bragged about in Noumea. Luckily for us he was OK on deck in the open air, and he managed to steer the boat for his three-hour watches. "He's a professional chef for crying out loud," I said to Leon, "and we're doing all the cooking!" Leon replied, "Show him how well you do in the galley, he may surprise us later."

As we approached the Great Barrier Reef at Capricorn Passage, great care was required in the strong rip tide over the shallower area and we cautiously worked our way through; the pass is very wide but not too much water under the keel. Inside the reef the surface became relatively smoother and remained flat for the next 280 miles as we made our way into our first Australian port, Mackay.

We tied up to the seawall and climbed 10 meters up a ladder to get to the dock, located the customs office and made the proper entry. The customs agent was very courteous and explained that all the fresh food remaining on board was to be confiscated by the Agriculture Department and disposed of.

He mentioned an eight meter tide and recommended we moved to a mooring buoy in the harbor for a few hours. We were a little disenchanted by our choice of landfall; this harbor is for large commercial ships only. We did not see any sailboats or a marina nearby and the nearest town is four miles away. We managed to get a few groceries at a nearby convenience store and we left promptly for Goldsmith Island, where we dropped anchor for the night.

We needed to reorganize ourselves and plan our visit to the Whitsunday Islands. We explored the fjords on Hook Island, and someone mentioned a great marina on Heyman Island, but when we arrived, we found the large marina was under construction and will be completed in the spring (November). We tied up to a city dock and enjoyed a pleasant shore excursion and our first meal in an Australian restaurant. Graham is going all out to introduce us to typical Australian cuisine.

This group of islands reminded me of the Virgins Islands—lots of good scuba diving and a large assortment of charter boats.

As we traveled north, the passage inside the Great Barrier Reef was well marked with numerous lighthouses. We stopped and anchored for a night at Fitzroy Island; next day we enter the Trinity River leading to Cairns. Here we first tasted Australian hospitality. The yacht club was very accommodating to visitors. Many of the transient boats were bound for Fremantle; there was *Scotch Mist*, *Nalu IV*, *Nicole*, *Providence II*, *Bounty* and *Genelle*. We spent an interesting fun week at the club, making new friends and planning for the next leg.

Leon asked me, "What are we going to do about Graham, he's a nice guy but we can't continue with him." I said, "Let me talk to him." Before I had a chance to say a word, Graham said to me, "I've enjoyed the trip, but my stomach can't get used to the motion of the boat. I still fell the boat moving under me, even when we're tied to the dock" I sympathized with him and suggested he might want to go home by plane, to which he agreed cheerfully. We never did taste any of his cooking! However, the captain of the *Genelle* knew a young lad that wanted to crew. At the club that evening, he introduced us to Joe, a pleasant young man who talked so fast we had a hard time keeping up with all he was saying about traveling for over a month in the outback of Northern Australia partly by bus and partly by hitchhiking. He was a sailing enthusiast; he knew the coastal area from Carnarvon to Rockingham, and that included Fremantle, our destination. I said to Leon, "Having someone who knows the local area on board could be very helpful." We enjoyed listening to his stories that evening and ask him to stop by the boat the next day.

We bid farewell to our new friends at the club and with Joe, our new companion, we started the trip north with a light easterly wind. A few days later we entered Albany Passage near the Cape York area. We anchored in a shallow bay facing Albany Island and the next morning we entered the very desolate Gulf of Carpenteria. Here we had the most incredible fishing experiences: no sooner did we put the fishing line in the water that within minutes we'd get a strike. Not wanting to freeze or waste any, we put the fishing line away after landing a fish. The next day we'd do the same again, we'd wet the line and get a fish within minutes. The bird life was correspondingly rife; we had a tern perched on the mizzen boom roosting there for the whole day. We tried giving him water and food but he declined and twelve hours later he just flew away. We hope he made it home OK.

I enjoy steering in the dark, gazing at the sky full of winking stars; I'm living the dream of a lifetime on this voyage and a night like this. It's medicine for the soul.

Having Joe with us on this trip made our life easier and he turned out to be a good deck hand, he even joined us in our daily yoga exercises; he's in better shape than we are and puts us to shame by purposely doing all sorts of intricate karate routines of his own. He can do the splits perfectly. We cannot compare his routine to what we do; amazing what 30 years' difference can make.

At Cape Wessel, we saw a Coast Guard vessel about a mile distant, just standing watch, not underway, and shortly after we had a small plane circling over us. They called on VHF and ask us to identify ourselves. Leon acknowledged and give then the needed information. They wished us a good day and a safe trip. As we approach Cape Don near Darwin, the water became murky; this area is treacherous because there are shoals extending well offshore and the currents are unpredictable. With the tide against us we carefully made progress into the port of Darwin. *Bounty* was already in port and calling us on the radio. The *Bounty*, by the way, is a beautiful Amel 45-foot ketch with a permanent hard dodger, a desirable feature that gives complete protection for the cockpit area, making her look more like a Motor Sailor. They wanted to know if we could join them for dinner. Every space in the harbor was occupied with fishing boats. We were grateful when one of the boats motioned that we could tie up alongside them and were able to join our friends for a pleasant evening and dinner at a brand new yacht club.

Darwin is a very modern city with brand new buildings everywhere; the city was completely rebuilt after the devastating Hurricane Tracy on Christmas Day 1974. Some parts of the city were still under construction. We saw three 12 meter boats on the deck of a cargo ship in the harbor. Leon walked over for a closer look and luckily he met the man in charge, who invited him aboard for a chat and a peek at Dennis Conner's *Stars and Stripes*, the *Eagle* and *Canada II*.

From Fiji to Darwin we covered 3,137 miles, and 11,274 miles from Fort Lauderdale. From here we will be sailing in company with the yacht *Bounty* and plan to keep radio contact twice a day for the final leg. We shall write you again from our next destination.

AU REVOIR!

Leon Simard
Leo Couturier

Hard Aground

 Heading north from Cairns with a good breeze and a moderate sea, we had great sailing along the coast and were averaging seven knots. We were enjoying the lively discussions with Joe, our new crew member, and more of his many stories about the difficult life he led while traveling in the Australian outback. He was pleased to have landed a ride on a yacht, thus avoiding going back home the way he had come.

The route between the Barrier Reef and the mainland gets narrower as you travel north; it is well marked with a series of lighthouses with fascinating names. They were supposedly named by Captain Cook 210 years ago. As we sailed past Lou Islet Light, Cape Tribulation, and the lights of Egret Reef, the wind gradually dropped but we still maintain a speed of five knots.

At 2.20 a.m. I was awakened by a frightening sound, as though we'd bumped against something. "I must be imagining things or having a dream," I thought. But then I heard it again. Crash! Bang! "Damn!" I said to myself. "We've touch bottom!" I shot up the companionway and within seconds I was standing next to Joe at the wheel.

"What was that?" I asked

"I don't know," he replied.

"We're in shallow water!" I shouted. As I looked up I could see the flash of a lighthouse dead ahead. "Holy shit," I thought, "he's aiming right for it, as if mesmerized!" We were so close I could see the structure of the lighthouse. I knew we were supposed to leave the lighthouse on our starboard so I grabbed the wheel from him and gave a hard turn to port to get away from the shallows. I looked at Joe and said, "You're supposed to call me when there are sightings!" I was about to ask him how come we were this close, but at that moment we jibed the mainsail and I shouted, "Wake up, Leon!" Immediately I heard Leon say, "I'm here, what do you need?"

He had gone to my bunk to wake me up after he heard the noise, and when he saw I wasn't there he rushed to the cockpit to find out what was going on.

"Let's take the headsail in!" I yelled in response. The headsail on *Blue Onyx* was a large genoa on a roller furling system. Joe snapped out of his inertia and started releasing the sheets as needed. I started the engine. Bang! We hit again! It seemed we'd come to a stop. Leon had finished with the headsail and move to the starboard side rail with a spotlight directed at the water. He was horrified by what was reflected back; we could see the bottom and there were rocks everywhere.

"We're still moving," Leon said.

I wanted to turn the boat another 60 degrees and head into the wind. I asked Joe, softly without shouting this time, to bring in the mainsail, but before we had time to turn, we hit again and this time we really stopped.

With Leon still shining the light on the starboard side, he said, "We're pressed against a big rock the size of a truck." I joined him to take a look, and what I saw was not a pretty sight. Again I put the boat in gear with a medium amount of throttle.

"She's not moving," said Leon. "Don't force it, we could do more damage to the boat. We're hard aground."

We finished rolling in the mainsail and we noticed the

boat was listing to starboard. I ask Joe to check the bilges. Looking where Leon's light was shining, we saw a few patches of sandy bottom on the port side, but the boat was totally surrounded by rocks.

"There's water above the floor in the galley," Joe reported.

I went below and engaged the clutch on the Jabsco bilge pump, which works off the engine belts, and promptly we had a good stream of water coming out at the stern. I began lifting the floor panels in front of the galley. I grabbed a flashlight and knelt on all fours in front of the sink area to see where the water was coming from and how much damage we had. I put on a diving mask and submerged the flashlight; surprisingly the light stayed on. I put my head under the water as low as I could and still couldn't see where the water was coming from. The pump was keeping the water level about the same.

I went back to the cockpit and told Leon, "I'll have to tear up the floor boards in front of the sink in order to get to the damaged area, and I may damage the beautiful teak and holly floor." That floor was such a source of pride for Leon, but without hesitation, he said, "It will be worse if we don't do it, so go ahead if you think we can stop the flooding. We have to keep the boat floating, otherwise we'll all have to swim."

Hearing those words made me feel terrible; suddenly I was conscious that we might lose the boat. I have delivered hundreds of boats over the years, but I have never felt as defeated and helpless as I did then. But I had to pull myself together and stop wasting time feeling sorry for myself. Leon was also mighty grim but remained fairly calm considering the situation we were in.

Most of the time I respond to situations with a confidence that I can fix anything, but at that point I wasn't too sure of where to start or what I was able to do. Naked to the waist, arms and shoulders covered with dirt, I was tearing up everything that was in the way. I got Joe to help me move everything out of the locker under the sink: there were pots and pans, cleaning materials, plastic bags full of odds and ends.

When we got to the bottom of the locker, I discovered under the tacky shelf paper that the bottom was not teak and holly after all, only a simple sheet of plywood secured with eight screws. Looking back, that made perfect sense, otherwise how could the boat be serviced? I removed the plywood and passed it to Joe.

Meanwhile Leon was on the radio trying to reach someone on channel 16, unable to raise any stations. "Is this radio working?" he asked. Then he tried the single sideband 2182 MHz marine frequency, again without success. I said, "I'll look at it later. I need to find what I'm looking for here first."

Then Leon said, "The pump is no longer working. It's probably clogged up." He told Joe to check the intake strainer for debris. Joe shone a light in the bilges and said, "The water's all gone!" "You're joking," I said, He handed me back the light so I could look for myself. First I shone it at the opening under me, as I had being dying to see what damage we had. There was still a small panel to remove and I quickly worked on that while Joe was getting more tools. Leon had already shut off the engine, and after I removed the obstructing plank I could see that part of the hull was bulging inward with a diagonal crack; the damaged area was approximately 10 by 20 centimeters, with one visible perforation the size of an AA battery. Also the sea cock valve next to it was bent at a strange angle. I saw no water coming in. That was peculiar.

"What time is it?" I asked Leon.

"It's 03:20. The tide is running out faster than we expected; we'll need to look at the tide table."

Shortly after, Leon had the tide book open to the right page and was looking at the tables.

"High water was at 23:06," he said, "and low tide will be 05:18."

"No wonder." I said, "The ocean water level is lower than the damaged part of the hull." The damage was approximately 30 centimeters. below the painted boot stripe. We began discussing what options we had and what could be done.

"We'll need to make some kind of patch on that hole to keep the water from coming in when the tide returns," Leon said, "and hopefully float the boat again."

We started scrounging around for materials for making repairs. Leon was in the forward cabin where we had a lot of stuff stored. No one had slept there since Gilles had left the boat. He came back with a bucketful of assorted gaskets, rubber mats and caulking materials. From two lockers I brought short pieces of lumber and wedges and a selection of tapered wooden plugs.

The cabin was now in total disarray with all the additional stuff we had spread everywhere. We discussed different scenarios and finally ended up placing two layers of dining-room placemats made of a light rubber material over the damaged area; on top of the mats we used a piece of hard plastic from the lid of a garbage pail, and two small blocks of wood stacked on top to fill the gap between the hull and the floor timber almost directly above the damaged area. Then we added two wooden wedges to keep everything in place. We did not dare to redress the bent sea cock for fear that it could break off completely. Instead we proceeded to place a generous amount of underwater putty (Marine Tex) that would harden in 20 minutes around the base, and hoped it would keep everything secured and in one solid mass. I said, "It's already 5.15 a.m. and we'll see what we are up against soon."

Daylight showed us a frightening sight; there was no water around the boat, only puddles and rocks everywhere. We put on rubber boots and climbed down to inspect the extent of the damage. There were a lot of scratches to the bottom paint on both sides of the keel and one large scratch higher up near the water line. There were no visible perforations. The shaft and propeller were not damaged; the rudder was scratched up and a chunk the size of a small saucer was missing on the lower edge. We checked the steering and that appeared to be working; the most damaged area was not visible because it was resting on that huge rock. I suspected that part of that rock was visible above water even at high tide.

We were walking in puddles, examining the path we came in and we found traces of red paint on some of the rocks we hit on the way in. It became evident that using the same way to get out was not an option. We walked around the boat in all directions; there appeared to be some deep water maybe 35 meters away in the direction the boat was now pointing. We returned to the boat and dragged the anchor and chain forward of the boat as far as we could and set the anchor in a sandy patch. I said, "This is where we have to bring the boat." On the way back to the boat, the water was coming in over my boots. "Hey! The tide is catching up," I said. "Let's keep moving, we still have a lot to do."

Back on the boat we planned our next move. Joe handed over some much welcomed sandwiches. Leon was back on the radio and this time someone answered on channel 16, advising us to switch to channel 72. Leon switched channels and gave them our position. "Three persons on board, no medical emergency and we are hard aground. Over."

We got a reply: "We are about 16 miles south of your position heading in your general direction; we should have you in sight in an hour, keep this frequency open." Knowing that we were not alone was a big relief.

"Even if they get here, they can't just come in here and pull us out," I told Leon. "They would damage their boat, and it would require over 100 meters of line to get to us. Those rocks will be invisible when they are covered and it's not a straight line to the deep water. We'll hit every rock on the way and if we get wedged between two boulders, we're toast. Somehow," I continued, "we have to show them the way. It's 07:10 and we could be afloat anytime after 10 a.m."

We were standing on the cabin top and I was pointing ahead, slightly to port. Leon said, "If we could weave our way to the left of those rocks…"

"But what about those two large rocks we walked by earlier?" Joe said. "We would need to pass between those two."

"You're right," I replied, "so here's the plan. Get me all those one-gallon water jugs that we have in the forward cabin, empty them, and attach a small line three meters long to each one. Remove all the weights from my scuba diving belt and attach one to the other end of each line. I'm going to scout the most probable channel to get through."

Then I took the extended boat hook in hand and I got in the water, half walking, half swimming; I used the boat hook to check the depth at different places and I returned to the boat. "How many buoys have we got?" I asked.

"We have five water jugs," said Joe.

"Good," I said, "I'll take the three that are ready and I'll need more. Take the small fender we use on the dinghy. How many more weights do we have?"

"Three," Joe said.

"Good. Put two weights on the fender buoy, because one may not be enough. We have a jug of olive oil in the galley as another possibility, and see what else you can find. If you need more weights, use some heavy tools from the toolbox."

Then I put on fins, mask and snorkel and started swimming away in one meter of water with the three buoys, looking for a possible path.

Watching me swimming away, Joe became very agitated and shouted to Leon, "Look! Look!" He was pointing at a shark at least two meters long, swimming slowly in the shallow water and in my direction. All they could do was call my name whenever they saw my head come out of the water, but with my head mostly submerged, I was unable to hear anything. Besides, I was too preoccupied looking for the first obstacle—a large boulder —that we had to avoid. When I found it, I placed a marker next to it then swam to the next boulder to place the second marker.

The next target was the narrow channel between two large boulders. There I placed the one remaining water-jug buoy on the right boulder and reserved the other side for the dinghy-fender buoy. I knew I had to remember that we would have to pass on the left of the buoys, or better still, keep them on our starboard side. Then I dragged the anchor chain to follow the path between the markers. Having been in the water a while I felt a little chilled; I finished adjusting the last buoy and swam back to the boat.

As I touched the rail I said, "Give me the others buoys if they're ready." Joe cut me off and said, "Get back on board, you need a break." Hearing that, I became annoyed and shouted, "Give me those darn buoys!" I took them right out of his hand and swam away, not wanting to be in the water any longer than necessary, and I hurried to find the channel and continue my work.

Back on board Joe and Leon were both shouting, "Leo! Leo!" They were unable to get my attention; I never did hear them.

"What can we do? said Joe. "I tried to warn him, though I didn't want to alarm him by screaming 'Shark! Shark!' But he wouldn't listen, and off he went."

"Leo is hard to cope with sometimes," answered Leon. "He's so stubborn."

"Oh no! Look over there, the shark is back and now there are two!"

Leon stared. "These are so much larger then the ones we see in the Bahamas!"

"What can we do?" Joe shouted. "We must do something!"

In the water, I was totally engrossed in the task at hand. I was also aware that there was lot more water to swim in, which meant that we could be afloat anytime. I found my passageway and quickly placed the larger dinghy-buoy across from the last one I'd placed earlier. Because it was bigger and could drift away, I wedge the double weights under a rock to make sure it was well secured. Suddenly I was aware of sea life around me, sponge-like plants attached to the rocks and colorful little fishes that were swimming nearby. For a moment I even thought, "I wonder if there are any lobsters about..." Not that I wanted to go fishing at a time like this.

I continued swimming further toward the deeper water with the other two buoys and placed them in a way to indicate the sandy patches we had seen earlier. As I secured the last marker, I recall thinking, "I hope I'll be able to remember all this correctly. Now I need to join the others back on the boat." Swimming on the surface in water that was five-and-a-half feet deep, I was breathing normally through the snorkel while checking the second-from-last buoy to make sure all was in place.

Suddenly, something hard hit me on the hip.

When anything touches you in an environment as remote as this, it is so unexpected that you immediately tense up. You try not to panic until you at least find out what it is. In a flash, I saw in the corner of my eye a large gray shape two feet from me.

Holy shit! Your mind goes through so many scenarios at lightning speed. "What was that?" I thought. And then my leg got bumped again. Without hesitation I propelled myself upward, and with my head high above water, I let out a scream.

To my surprise it was our dinghy that had bumped against my leg, and I saw Leon with his arm extended toward me. I grabbed his hand, glad to see him nearby since I was beginning to feel cold and exhausted. Before I had a chance to take a breath, he grabbed under my arm with his other hand and pulled me up so hard and fast that I shouted, "Hey! Take it easy!" But by then, I was already in the bottom of the boat. Leon said, "You scared me to death!"

"I'm OK," I said, " I got the channel all marked out."

"Never mind that!" He proceeded to tell me about the sharks circling about. "I thought for sure you were a goner."

"What are you talking about? If there were sharks I would have seen them."

At that very moment Leon shouted, "Look, look!"

Looking where he was pointing I could see both sharks

swimming right between the two buoys I had just installed moments ago.

"I can't believe what I'm looking at," I gasped, and started shaking uncontrollably. I wasn't sure if it was from the fear or the cold—probably both. Leon started rowing back toward the boat. The early sun felt good on my wet and tired body. Looking down I saw the two sharks again, slowly swimming parallel to us, probably wondering where that odd-looking fish had gotten to.

"Boy," I said to Leon, "am I glad you came to pick me up. I could have been their lunch!"

Just then I looked up and saw a 25-meter fishing-trawler-type boat near the deep water area. I waved at them and they waved back. They were dropping an anchor when we arrived at our boat. Joe said, "We have company coming." Three men in a dinghy were now underway in our direction. They lost no time approaching our crippled boat and we asked them to come aboard, exchanged greetings and introduced ourselves to the trawler's captain, mate and engineer.

We explained all that had happen to us in the last 10 hours. The trawler captain said, "We wanted to see if the vessel can be floated free and to assess the extent of damages. Before we go further we need to set salvage fees."

We were taken aback with that line of talk; it appears we had a different kind of shark on board our vessel. Quickly I switched to French and said to Leon, "If we allow them to put a line on your boat, they can claim half or more of the value of the boat from your insurance company. We need to know what the captain has in mind."

"Ask him outright what he wants," Leon replied.

So I asked the captain if he had a Lloyd Open Form contract. He said, "No, I don't have contract forms."

I then told Leon, "A Lloyd Open Form contract is a document that says right on the contract 'No cure, no pay,' and without such a document, regular salvage laws generally apply." Then I asked the captain what price he intended to charge for the salvage so I could advise the owner.

"Does that mean you're ready to agree on salvage?" he said.

I could hardly blame the trawler's captain for wanting to exploit the situation; I just wanted him to show his hand but by now I was thinking that he might want to get underway if he didn't have some sort of agreement.

"No, actually…I'd like to make you an offer," I replied. "We're very happy you are here and I definitely want you to stay; unfortunately you can't just come in here to pull us out without endangering your ship. I know it's a big gamble, but we have a small window of time that will give us a chance to get out of here at high tide through the channel we marked. I will pay you $1000 to stand by for two hours and, if we don't succeed, we'll talk about salvage, because by then the situation will have changed dramatically. In your case you win a little or you win a lot. Is that OK with you?"

Leon was standing by the engine controls and announced, "It's 10 o'clock, and we need to move on with our plans."

Our visitors agreed to our proposal. They wished us luck and returned to their boat; we ask them to keep channel 72 on the radio open.

I explained to Joe and Leon that we had to keep all the water-jug buoys on our starboard side. But the fender buoy had to be passed on our port side. Joe grabbed the spinnaker pole and lowered one end against the bottom and tried to push us away from the rock. "Give me a hand, maybe if we all push..." he said. Leon and I joined him, and with the three of us leaning hard on the pole, Joe shouted, "Keep pushing! We've moved a little, come on, push!" And sure enough we were now clear of that rock.

Leon yelled, "We're afloat, let's go for it!" He grabbed the wheel and I took a position at the bow to see down the channel and give directions. Joe retrieved the spinnaker pole and placed it in its chocks on the deck, Leon put the boat in gear and slowly we were moving ahead.

After a short run, I pointed 20 degrees to port and was pulling in the anchor chain as fast as I could. The water pump was on again with a good flow astern; we were still flooding. I wondered if it was the hole we covered or another hole somewhere else.

Moments later we passed our first buoy, then the second buoy. Now we had to turn to starboard and pass between the next two markers. We were heading dead center through our channel when we touched bottom. Looking down I didn't see anything. Leon leaned over on one side and Joe the other. They both said they could see no rocks, that it looked like sandy bottom.

"I'll try giving it more power," said Leon. He engaged the gears, opened the throttle, and the boat moved a little.

"Keep it going," Joe said, and with a few more scrapes we gathered speed, passed the other two buoys and were finally in deep water.

"Hooray!" we shouted, looking at each other with disbelief. But now we could sink if the pumps couldn't keep up. Leon steered for the trawler while I secured the anchor and went below to check on the leak. A lot of water was coming in and the pumps were keeping the bilges half full. We tied up alongside the trawler and the captain invited us aboard to meet the rest of the crew.

"You had a good plan," he said, "and I'm glad you made it." He then came aboard our boat and we showed him the temporary repairs we had made. After discussing possible eventualities, the captain suggested that I tap in the wooden wedges to secure the blocks of wood so they didn't get loose and fall out. That seemed a good idea, and when I tapped the wedges in a little more, to our surprise the leak shrank to barely a trickle.

Over a nice lunch the cook had prepared for us, they complimented us on getting out of that horrible situation without help and admitted that they had not shared our confidence and were getting ready to go into action. We appreciated the lunch, thanked them for waiting as agreed, and paid the captain the $1000. And, given the ordeal we'd just been through, not to mention the huge pile of stuff in our now nonfunctional galley, that was probably the best money we spent on a meal during the entire voyage.

Then we told the captain about the rudder, and that we would like to have a good look at the bottom to see what other damage we might have. He told us about a nice protected bay nearby with a sloping beach where local fishermen went to careen their boats. "You could safely ground your vessel there," he said, "and do some repairs at low tide." The crew showed us on the charts where it was located and asked if we needed any tools or materials. Meanwhile Joe had gone with one of their men in their dinghy to pick up all the water-jug buoys and weights. As we pulled away from their sturdy vessel, Leon said, "What a nice bunch of men they turned out to be."

Less than one hour later we found the little bay and we managed to beach the boat on its port side using padding and braces as best we could with what materials we had available. Later that afternoon we had visitors: our friends from the trawler entered the bay, dropped anchor and dragged a large cooler full of Foster beer to the beach.

"Hi, mate!" one of them shouted. "How are you making out?" They handed me a bottle of beer. Looking at the size of the bottle I said, "I'll get some glasses—that's family size. We'll share this one."

He said, "Nonsense mate, that's Aussie size." It was at least three-quarters of a liter or more! He handed one each to Joe and Leon. We all sat on the beach talking while the tide kept going out. When they offered me a second beer, they found me spread out on the sand, sound asleep, and when I awakened the tide was up and our boat was afloat again.

I said, "You should have woken me up."

"We tried..." they said, and they all laughed.

"What about the rudder?" I asked.

"All done," the captain said. "She's as good as new, mate."

The Australian crew had worked with Joe and Leon; they managed to sand the damaged area properly and applied a generous amount of Marine Tex to the rudder and gave the same treatment to the hole under the sink.

Nineteen hours had elapsed since we'd gone aground, but to me it felt like an eternity. I couldn't shake the memory of this horrible experience. We could have lost the boat, ruined the entire trip, and altered all our lives. I dreaded the thought of what would have happened if the grounding had taken place at high tide. We were very fortunate to have so little damage thanks to everyone's valiant efforts and our good fortune to have the trawler standing by. In a way, I'm almost sorry we cheated them out of the salvage!

Early next morning, with everyone in the trawler's galley having coffee and looking over charts, their crew showed us where to engage a safe passage across the top of Australia. "Follow the coast till you get to Cape North," the captain told us, "then go on a westerly course [276 degrees] for the Gulf of Carpenteria. You'll avoid going up the Torres Strait with its currents and heavy traffic. You'll have good water under the keel till you get to Cape Don near Darwin."

From Darwin to Fremantle

Nine days later, and with no further incidents, we sailed into the harbor at Darwin. The city of Darwin, 1,916 miles from our next destination, Fremantle, is known unofficially as the capital of Northern Australia. While in Darwin we shared many sea stories with the crew of the fishing boat tied up next to us in the harbor. They were a lively bunch and we invited them to join us for dinner to introduce them to our friends on *Bounty*, Murray and Ken. We were still traveling together, keeping in radio contact as we headed toward Fremantle.

Murray owned three fishing trawlers and, surprisingly, our guests turned out to be good friends of two of the three skippers working for Murray. The day we left Darwin they gave us two kilos of shrimps for us to enjoy on the way. *Blue Onyx* and *Bounty* slid out of the harbor together with the tide running in our favor this time. When we got to the Sea of Timor the wind disappeared completely, leaving us with a mirror-like surface to travel on. We had to motor for the next two days.

Our daily exchanges on the radio worked well, and we teased *Bounty* about the distance between us increasing by 12 miles a day. (Our longer water line gave us a speed advantage.) The northerly wind returned to give us a good sail for the following five days, only to disappear again, and this time we did not dare use the engine because we didn't relish entering the Indian Ocean low on fuel.

Leon told Murray, "We'll have to go to Dampier [a coastal town 45 miles due east] and get fuel."

"I'm 68 miles behind you," Murray responded, "and we're also low on fuel. My boats happen to be fishing near this area, so I'm making arrangements to rendezvous with Captain Lou on the *Kingfisher* and get fuel from him." The *Kingfisher* carried 12,000 gallons of fuel so could easily give us the 80 or so gallons we each required.

Blue Onyx met up with the *Kingfisher* and we had a coffee in their wheelhouse. Then one of their crew passed a hose across the deck to our boat and we gratefully filled our fuel tanks. We motored southward for four more hours and the wind gradually returned to give us a good sailing day. Ten hours later, Murray caught up with *Kingfisher* and got the fuel he needed.

By now we were finding the waves to be unusually high for this little amount of wind. "The Indian Ocean is renowned for having big waves," Murray explained over the radio. "It's a deep ocean with no high land or islands to reduce the fetch."

The further south we traveled, the colder it got at that time of year. The winds were only 20 miles an hour, but the waves were sending walls of water and spray clear across the boat. We were bouncing and falling off steep wave tops to hit the surface at the bottom of the wave as though it was solid ground. What a difference from the calm seas we had two days earlier! Everyone was exhausted from just hanging on; the larger waves were hitting the side of the boat, and slowing our progress. The wind was not letting up and we shortened sails. We knew there wouldn't be any sleep again that night.

Then I surprised Leon with his famous one-liner and said, "IT MUST BE PLAIN HELL ASHORE ON A NIGHT LIKE THIS!" Leon laughed out loud and agreed.

The next day we had a whale as big as our boat keeping us company, swimming first on one side of us, then the other. From its perspective, we may have appeared to be one of its peers. We hoped it didn't intend to try to mate with the boat. Joe wasn't doing well; he was suffering and was retching over the side every hour. He stayed topside to be close to the rail and was getting soaked every time a wave hit the side of the boat. We told him to stop chumming or we would feed him to the whale. That bit of humor relieved our anxiety and we felt confident that conditions would soon improve.

Halfway through my watch, I was pushed to leeward and hit my head on the cockpit winch. I don't know how long I lay on the cockpit floor. I had difficulty undoing the buckle on my harness, but I managed to crawl on all fours to wake up Leon. I told him I was not feeling well and had to lie down; he took one look at my face covered with blood from a cut on the right side of the head and jumped out of bed.

"What happened to you?" he said, startled. Joe helped him carry me to my bunk; they cleaned me up and bandaged the side of my head. Leon said to Joe, "He probably got knocked down when the boat rolled off a steep wave— there's blood everywhere in the cockpit." Joe recommended going ashore to the nearest town for medical help.

"Unfortunately the wind is directly from that direction," said Leon. "Better to continue sailing south and let him rest. We'll check on him periodically." "I slept till morning, then came up on deck to do my watch. "So what happens when you're scared half-to-death twice?" said Leon. "First the whale gave me a fright, and now you! You don't look too good. Go get more rest. Joe's better, so we can share your watch for now."

It started to rain and I did not need more persuading to return to my bunk. Later that afternoon I joined the others in the cockpit and we contacted Murray on the radio.

It turned out they had run into the same conditions 90 miles behind us. That morning they had had a problem with the jib not staying attached to the head stay; they had had a hard time changing sail because of the bad conditions. With only the two of them on board, they were exhausted. We felt compelled to encourage them somehow. We told them that the rain had flattened the waves considerably in our area and that their conditions would improve soon.

Not long after, Leon remarked to Joe, "Now, the compass isn't working—it's gone crazy." I remembered reading somewhere that when you travel in the Southern Hemisphere, funny things happen to some compasses. The magnetic field near the North Pole activates compasses, and we compensate for that with little magnets installed within the compass housing. Therefore, when you travel to the Southern Hemisphere, the adjustments made in the Northern Hemisphere no longer apply and in fact have an adverse effect. I didn't want to work on recalibrating the compass at that time, so we sailed by observing the "course over ground" on the sat-nav. The next morning we saw land on the port bow and we sailed parallel to the coast, making shorter tacks to stay in sight of the land. During the night, we favored the port tack to keep us well offshore.

The next day, we called *Bounty* to let them know we could see the city of Fremantle ahead of us. Murray said, "Am I glad to hear good news for a change. The weather here has improved and by tomorrow this time we should be where you're at now." We agreed to call every two hours to make sure they were OK, but mostly we wanted them to know they still had company even if we were about to enter the harbor.

Then we dressed ship by hoisting a string of flags from the masthead to the bow and stern of the vessel and, with Joe recognizing familiar landmarks, he directed us safely to the Fremantle Sailing Club's dock.

Tired and awash in pride, we exchanged hugs, and with big smiles on our faces, we received congratulations from the club secretary and a few club members who greeted us at the dock. "You are the first foreign private yacht to arrive," said the secretary. "We get calls every day about boats coming to attend the America's Cup Special Event." It turned out that every marina and yacht club in Fremantle was preparing for the thousands of boats expected in the next few months.

"The time is 10.20 a.m. on August 30," I said to Leon. "We're two days ahead of the September 1st predicted date of arrival!" Leon had worked hard to accomplish this trip. He had successfully sailed his own boat every mile of the way to Australia and earned the admiration of everyone at the Fremantle club, as well as back home in Quebec.

The next day when the *Bounty* entered the harbor, we rushed over to help catch her lines and secure the boat; we hugged, shook hands all around, and headed for the bar.

During our time in Fremantle, Joe was a big help, introducing us to neat places and many of his friends. We became full members of the Fremantle Sailing Club and proceeded to haul out the boat to do proper repairs and touch up the topside paint.

Michel and his girlfriend, Frances, arrived from their travels in New Zealand and eastern Australia; they would be taking over the operation of the boat and staying with *Blue Onyx* for the coming season. As for me, my delivery contract had been completed and I would be going back to Montreal with Leon, although I returned to Australia when the racing finals took place.

Leon made several visits back and forth in the ensuing five months. Michel and Frances worked on *Blue Onyx* during that time, entertaining many guests from Canada and Europe, and saw the biggest racing event in Australian history. Meanwhile, Michel had purchased a 30-foot sloop, which he named *Pax*, and began planning for the long journey home. When the races finished, he and Frances began a 14-year adventure sailing and working all over the world, including the Philippines, Japan, Singapore, the Suez Canal, the Mediterranean, South America and Hawaii. They finally arrived home in Vancouver, Canada, in 2001. They still live on board their beloved little *Pax* and are planning to sail back to Australia soon.

In March 1987, Leon sold *Blue Onyx*. He was now 68, and having completed the trip of a lifetime, decided to divest himself of the responsibilities of boat ownership and instead charter boats when he wanted to sail. It was the end of a special era for us, but I continue to this day to sail with the Simards from time to time.

Shopping for Antique Boats

 In 1997, while I was working at the Sunseeker dealership in Pompano Beach, Florida, delivering boats, a man from Brazil, Marcos de Moraes, purchased a brand new, 80-foot Sunseeker Manhattan powerboat and hired me as full-time captain. After I'd spent a year on the job, Marcos began showing me listings he'd received from a yacht broker of some large, pre-owned sailboats and said he'd like to buy an antique sailboat and restore it.

"Those boats look good in the photos," I said, "but the restoration of antique boats is a complicated, time-consuming undertaking. Not a good idea to get involved in this. If you want to sail, buy yourself a brand new Swan or a Hinckley, something you could enjoy immediately. How much sailing have you done in the past?"

He avoided answering my question and said instead, "If I had a choice, I would like to do what you are doing."

I said to myself, "He must mean he would like the freedom to sail the seas as I do."

Every other week he would show me more listings from Europe and ask, "What do you think of these beauties?"

"Before you buy anything like that, I said, "you'd better get someone that is critically impartial about them or you'll get royally screwed."

"That's why I want you to go look at them," he said.

Two days later, I was on a plane to La Spezia, Italy. I was meeting with a yacht broker from England named Mike to visit the *Orion*, a 130-foot gaff rig ketch of 1928 vintage. Captain Ignacio gave us a grand tour of the vessel and we found her to be in remarkable condition for a boat her age; but he told us the boat required a minimum crew of 12. I couldn't see anyone wanting to go that route, especially not my boss, who, I had learned, had never done any sailing before.

The next day Mike took me to the port of San Stefano to visit the *Black Swan*, a120-foot 1899 sloop. Her profile and appearance were spectacular. Captain Edmond Pecchiolli said, with pride, "This is a true classic. In two years she will be 100 years old." I completed my inspection, thinking to myself. "This boat urgently needs a complete refit, immediately, if they want to make the century mark." Even the broker was disappointed, but insisted that I go to Spain to see the other two vessels he had proposed.

I took a plane to Barcelona and caught up with Captain Mike Pope, who showed me the 140-foot, 1934 *Sylvia*. The first thing I asked him was, "Why is the boat sitting so high above her water lines?"

"They removed a large amount of lead ballast to do a restoration project," he said, "and stored the ballast at the yard to be picked up later." The captain and his wife were the only crew remaining on board. After we inspected the vessel together, I took the captain and his wife ashore and, over dinner, I learned the history of the vessel.

Restoration had started four years ago, but none of the projects had been completed, mainly due to the owner's lack of funds. The boat had sat for years and the money never came. Eventually the boat changed hands and Mike had come aboard to finish the work in progress and make the boat operational again. The sudden death of her new owner two months earlier changed everything. Mike had not received his salary for nine weeks and would be leaving the boat unless something positive happened soon.

Then he added, "If you want to do a sea trial I could find enough crew among friends in the harbor to sail her for a few hours. And could you advance $1,200 to collect the sails that were left at the sail maker for repairs? That would be discounted from the purchase price, of course."

I didn't want to ask how much he owed the boatyard for the incomplete work and for the marina's dockage. Well aware of Mike's desperation, I wished I could give him hope, but all I could tell him was, "Try not to use your own resources on this boat."

The next day I visited a 1939, 96-footer called *Sea Gypsy* in Palma de Mallorca. Captain Jeff Engholm was expecting me and together we looked in every possible corner. I found this boat well maintained and in good working condition compared to the previous three and told him so.

I returned home and wrote four reports describing each vessel, with numerous recommendations. I wrote that *Sea Gypsy* was the only one worth considering as a feasible project. I felt an immense responsibility. I was 65 when Marcos hired me the previous year, and although Marcos was a very successful entrepreneur, he was only 28 years old, married and the father of two baby boys. I was very concerned about his desire to buy a two-to-four-million-dollar antique boat and get involved with a restoration project.

One week later, I was shocked when Marcos called me and said, "*Sea Gypsy* is too small for my family and crew. I made an offer on *Black Swan* and she is being surveyed this week. We'll need to go back for a sea trial next Wednesday."

Captain Pecchiolli welcomed the three of us as Mike the broker, my boss and I stepped aboard; we stood on the aft deck while they motored away from shore. Half an hour later Mike was talking with Captain Pecchiolli and he came over to us and said, "There's hardly any wind, we'll not bother raising the sail." I told him, "We flew here all the way from Brazil and Miami for a sea trial and you will put up sail if you want any chances of selling this boat."

With a lot of agitated talk in Italian, the crew began raising the sails and it became obvious that only the captain was familiar with the boat. The eight crew members were not regular crew and they were tripping over each other with no idea what to do next. We stood there in disbelief. I counted 92 minutes to raise the mainsail and 26 more minutes to raise the jib. By then we had a bit of wind, but we found the boat was very tender even with this little wind. When asked about this, they told us that a new, taller mast had been installed to improve performance. But this meant she was better suited to sheltered waters rather than ocean work. The next day, the surveyor handed us a 31-page report that revealed she had failed the survey badly. We returned to Miami and the next day got a call from Mike. "They won't accept that we're refusing the boat," he said, "and they came up with a counter offer."

"I think we can get it for a real good price," said Marcos.

That is when I lost my cool. I told him, "I don't care if you buy a one-million- or a four-million-dollar boat. You pay me regular wages, but if you want to listen to Mike regarding this boat..." I stared hard at him and jokingly I added, "What you need is a good kick in the pants."

We both burst out laughing and that was the end of *Black Swan*. We had discussed chartering sailboats before and I mentioned this again, explaining that this would help Marcos make sure what it was he wanted and—above all—what he didn't want. Marcos agreed and we chartered a Swan, the Rolls Royce of sailboats, out of St. Maarten. Two days later he said, "This is too modern-looking." Then we chartered *Endeavor*, a 140-foot 1934 J-Class boat owned by Elizabeth Meyers, which was taking part in Antigua Race

Week. This one met with his approval but it was not for sale at the time. (However, she was sold a year later to Dennis Kozlowski, the infamous tycoon later convicted of stealing millions from Tyco, the company he headed.)

Then we heard there was a similar boat available in Newport, and the following week I was looking at *Shamrock V*, a 130-foot 1930 J Class. The sail maker had delivered a new mainsail that day and was making minor adjustments. When the boat was properly trimmed, the captain let me have the wheel. Let me tell you, I do not care how many fine boats you have sailed before: to experience the perfection of a 164-ton boat doing 14 knots in a relatively light wind with her decks at a slight angle, well-balanced and stable as a locomotive—that was an unbelievable experience. I called my boss and said, "We've found the boat for you. You need to come here and see for yourself." A few days later we arranged for another sea trial and, with very little negotiation, Marcos soon owned the boat.

I returned to Newport for the survey. The boat was in remarkably good condition; we found 6 by 30 centimeter teak planks on the topside measuring between 8 and 13 meters long. You can't buy lumber like that anymore. The planks were attached with bronze bolts to steel frames and the frames were not even rusted. Thomas Perry was hired as captain, as he had the experience and a better understanding of how to handle the J boats.

He and a crew of seven began preparations for a trip to the Caribbean. When the boat was ready, Marcos invited me to accompany him as a guest and we shared the most incredible sail to Antigua. We congratulated each other on finding such a fine vessel. Not having the responsibility of the boat, I was able to relax and enjoyed watching all the operations. I was feeling so good that, early one morning during my yoga exercise on the foredeck, I surprised everyone by climbing on the boom to do a headstand while the boat was moving at 14 knots!

The decision to rebuild *Shamrock V* came after the Antigua Classic Regatta, during which she took the honors from another J-Class yacht, the *Valsheda*. We hired the naval architect guru of J boats, Gerry Dijkstra, as project manager and he arranged for Pendennis Shipyard in Falmouth, U.K., to undertake a complete restoration.

Shamrock V was launched 20 months later: she had been the last of the remaining three J boats to receive a complete refit. In August 2001, she joined the America's Cup Jubilee Celebrations in England, which starred the three leading J boats. *Valsheda* was presented by her owner, Ronald de Waal of Holland. *Endeavour* was there with her then-owner, Dennis Kozlowski, and *Shamrock V* made her debut with Marcos de Moraes. These three boats were meeting again for the first time in 65 years.

Marcos presented me with a large original framed photo of *Shamrock V* with this message written on the back: "Dear Leo and Christine, Here is a picture of your 'godchild' *Shamrock V*. We are sure that we all will enjoy many wonderful days on board her in the future."

To Marcos I want to say, I admire you for your passion and wisdom in bringing this magnificent yacht back to her former glory. I cherished the time we spent together and I'm glad you're out there sailing as you desired. By gosh, you're doing it in style. You're cool!

A Word from the Captain's Wife

 A girl in every port?

He loves to tell everyone that "We met in a bar where all the sailors hang out." My version is a bit more dignified—after all, I was in Nassau on a business trip for a rather conservative Fortune 500 company, and did not make a habit of frequenting bars. Besides, not having set foot on a sailboat prior to meeting Leo makes it even more improbable that I would have been on the prowl for mariners!

But the attraction between us that evening was undeniable, and our initial encounter set the tone for a courtship that unfolded in some of the world's most beautiful and exotic sailing destinations. My first idyllic day-sail in Fort Lauderdale; the blur of Bermuda pastels as we traversed the island by moped; a crash course in radar readings on a foggy July night in Bar Harbor, Maine; the glitz and glamour of Newport; and an introduction to his lively siblings in Montreal—all deepened my feelings toward "Captain Leo."

From our very first conversations, though, I learned that this fascinating man was preparing for a year-long contract to sail the *Blue Onyx* to Australia for the America's Cup Challenge. And as the months leading up to the start of this odyssey sped by, I became more and more determined that I would be his girl in every port!

We spent the year-end holidays together in Fort Lauderdale, just a month prior to his departure. It was a bittersweet time: the excitement of the upcoming adventure was mingled with the dread of separation and the anxiety of the unknown. The marriage license we took out during that time simply got folded and put away. And as we parted, I desperately clung to the adage that "if you love someone, set him free…if he comes back, it's meant to be."

We were not, in any event, going to lose touch. I had persuaded Leo to use my apartment as his "permanent" US address; he had briefed me on how we would communicate via ham radio; and I had already masterfully scheduled my next business trip to Panama to coincide with the arrival of *Blue Onyx* in Colón. So, less than a month after she had set sail from Fort Lauderdale, I was again on board this magnificent Hinckley, acting as the requisite fifth crew member for the Panama Canal crossing. It was a marvelous experience, the day ending with a special celebratory dinner on the Pacific side.

But before we knew it, Leo and I were again saying our goodbyes. This time, having no planned rendezvous in sight, I was distraught as the door closed behind him. A few minutes later, a knock sent my heart soaring—no, he'd not returned for one last kiss, but the bouquet he'd ordered delivered to my room sealed my determination not to allow this man to "sail off into the sunset" for good.

And so began months of waiting for those wonderful chronicles and occasional pictures to arrive; but—more importantly—for the phone to ring and to hear some stranger's voice saying, "I've got Leo on the line—let me patch you through." Our conversations always began with a reading of the boat's coordinates, which I would plot onto a world map as soon as we'd hung up. We would talk briefly, always conscious that there could be numerous sets of ears tuning in.

As *Blue Onyx* distanced herself further from the Americas, those precious calls came in at ever more bizarre hours, yet they were as welcomed as ever. By April I began to hatch a plan to meet up with the "captain of my heart" in Fiji. The logistics would be much more complex than our encounter in Panama: I couldn't exactly justify the trip to Fiji as a business necessity since my assigned territory was Latin America and the Caribbean; nor could I rely on having the *Blue Onyx* sail in to Fiji precisely when I would be there.

But I was not to be deterred, and in June I made the marathon trip from Pennsylvania to Suva, in the Fiji Islands. Much to my dismay, *Blue Onyx* was not in port when I arrived, and as there was no way for me to make contact with Leo, I now faced the real possibility that my plans for a reunion would unravel. Thirty-six long hours later, I finally heard the voice on the other end of the line saying these sweet words: "Hi, honey, we're here!"

Our reunion was as passionate as the setting was exotic. Obviously, time and distance were doing nothing to diminish our feelings for one another. And when Leo presented me with a stunning black pearl pendant that he'd selected in Bora Bora, it was a tangible expression of the longings we'd shared over the previous four months.

The absurd length of corporate vacations being what they are, it seemed as though I was on a plane heading back to the United States in the blink of an eye. This parting was no easier than the others, and—once again—I was faced with the uncertainty of where, when, and how we would manage to see one another.

A few weeks later, when a ham operator based in Anchorage, Alaska, patched Leo through in the wee morning hours, the static on the line could not dampen the exhilaration we felt from a conversation that went something like this:

Leo: "Do you remember what we've talked about doing?" – OVER –

Me: "Yes, of course!" – OVER –

Leo: "Well, what are the requirements to do it in Pennsylvania?" – OVER –

Me: "I don't know, but I'll find out tomorrow!" – OVER –

And so, in coded form, I had just received a marriage proposal from aboard a sailboat over 8,000 miles away!

Planning a wedding under any circumstance can be challenging, but doing so knowing that the groom would be returning to North America only one week prior to the big day in October—and then would depart a week later to complete his contract in Australia—made this an extraordinary experience. While to others it may have seemed a peculiar way to begin a marriage, to us it was yet another manifestation that our lives together would be a nomadic adventure.

Today, as we approach 20 years since this corporate type tied the knot with a certified old salt, Leo still delights in responding to that perennial question, "Is it true that sailors have a girl in every port?" by quipping, "How should I know? I haven't been to every port!"

Legacy

Have you ever been to sea?

I listen to the sound of waves on the side of the boat; I remember life on board and wish I could do it all over again. There is a magical sense of romance and adventure about going to sea for amusement or earning a living that gives you the courage to surmount the challenges of living on a small boat.

When I began doing deliveries, I was working at a boat-yard, living on my little wooden sloop and delivering boats part-time. The mere fact that I was always available to do a delivery made me popular with the brokers, and I would turn down a more lucrative local job to accept a delivery job, often for less money or no compensation at all. I would drop whatever I was doing and sail the boat to the desired destination. Eventually these activities turned into full-time work And so it was that I embarked on a career at sea and I have never regretted making that decision.

I want to thank all the bright young men and women who came aboard as my crew, because none of the above would have happened without their valiant efforts and dedication to our endeavors. They became my best friends and I am proud to know that eight of my former crew became professional captains themselves, and there are probably a few others with whom I've lost contact who did as well.

I also owe a great deal of gratitude to the Simard family, especially to Jean, Arthur and Leon as they were my prime clients for 26 years; and also to Marcos de Moraes; they have given me the opportunity to manifest my love for the sea and to travel on the most elaborate yachts imaginable.

And I want to say, "Thanks for all those years that I have sailed first-class with my best pals (all my clients) who trusted me to steer their yachts to incredible places. I know some of you realized that I never did it for the money. I will always remember the good times we shared and I would do it all over again."

I ran into Michel in Montreal recently and I asked him, "Why did you always say yes when I called and ask you to crew?" Then I asked him to write out his response so I could include it in this book. Here is what he wrote:

Salut Leo!

You asked: "Why did you always say yes?"
Here is my reply:
"Yes, I must confess, Leo was my first..."
  The *Neslein*, *Dramis*, *Mal de Terre*, *Madame Butterfly*,
     Midnight Sun, *Dolphin*, *Blue Onyx* and a few others
     somewhere...
I have sailed all of them under his command.
From learning to tie a proper knot,
To raising and reefing a sail, steering a course by the stars
     and the feel of the wind on your neck,
From reading the color of the water and its depth and
     learning how to anchor securely,
From the first time out of sight of land, first overnight and
     landing in a foreign port.
Learning how to work out a fix with a sextant and
     raising land after an ocean crossing.
From learning of the sea, its silences and furies,

Its patience and seriousness, its vastness and our smallness.

From the longhaired wannabe drifting Kerouac to the bald-
ing close-cropped sea nomad many waves later.

Because there was always the promise of romance and
adventure

Of limitless horizons, unknown and unpredictable

Always in style, with flair and panache;

How could I have turned down a berth every time
Leo offered me one?

And if I do have a sparkle in my eyes, a walk and
strut with a jaunt in my step sometimes

And if I can sniff the wind and charm my way into some
favorable wake somewhere

Yes, yes I am glad to confess, "Leo was my first..."

With respect and affection to Leo my sensei-skipper

Michel

Epilogue

 Recreational boating is a 70-billion-dollar-a-year business. For three decades, I've been fortunate to be able to do what most people dream of doing once in their lifetime. But the average captain today is aged anywhere from 45 to late 60s; to me, that says there are not enough young people attracted to this growing industry.

How would you like a job that not only pays well, but provides all-expenses-paid adventures to some of the world's most exotic destinations—or, a job on a boat making local trips, allowing you to go home every night? With this book, I've tried to provide enough information to allow you to take advantage of the unlimited opportunities in the marine industry. Boats over 17 meters require crew and support personnel—mechanics, technicians, cooks, entertainers, and service-oriented persons in general. So get yourself on board any vessel. As you gain experience, you'll soon develop the confidence you need to succeed.

As for me, forty years after I first set sail, I've now returned home to Canada because I became allergic to too much sun. Getting old is OK...as long as you can still embrace the thrills of tomorrow! So I've joined the Mimico Cruising Club in Toronto; although I don't have a boat at present, I hear the Trent-Severn River Waterway to Georgian Bay in Ontario is a most spectacular place to cruise. Don't be surprised if you see me there helping some boat owners next summer!

Happy sailing!